EDUCATION QUALITY MANAGEMENT

Education Quality Management

EFFECTIVE SCHOOLS THROUGH SYSTEMIC CHANGE

Jerry J. Herman, Ph.D.

PROFESSOR OF ADMINISTRATION AND PLANNING
COLLEGE OF EDUCATION
THE UNIVERSITY OF ALABAMA

Janice L. Herman, Ph.D.

ASSOCIATE PROFESSOR
DEPARTMENT OF EDUCATIONAL LEADERSHIP
SCHOOL OF EDUCATION
THE UNIVERSITY OF ALABAMA AT BIRMINGHAM

TECHNOMIC
PUBLISHING CO., INC.
LANCASTER · BASEL

Education Quality Management

a **TECHNOMIC**®publication

Published in the Western Hemisphere by
Technomic Publishing Company, Inc.
851 New Holland Avenue, Box 3535
Lancaster, Pennsylvania 17604 U.S.A.

Distributed in the Rest of the World by
Technomic Publishing AG
Missionsstrasse 44
CH-4055 Basel, Switzerland

Printed in the United States of America
10 9 8 7 6 5 4 3 2 1

Main entry under title:
   Education Quality Management: Effective Schools Through Systemic Change

A Technomic Publishing Company book
Bibliography: p. 179
Index: p. 187

Library of Congress Catalog Card No. 94-60073
ISBN No. 1-56676-138-7

To four very special people
who exhibit excellent listening and feedback skills,
and who exemplify the best traits of caring and helping human beings —
Nellie, Geebo, Norma, and Donald John, we thank you and
we love you for who you are and for the values we all should hold.

WHY WAS THIS BOOK WRITTEN?

THIS book was written for multiple purposes. First, it intends to explain the basics of the newest program that is being introduced into school districts from the field of business—that of Total Quality Management. Secondly, it utilizes Quality Management as a catalyst to integrate change, which combines other current programs being implemented in schools with Quality Management's structure and processes. Thirdly, it develops a systemic planning model that utilizes all of these sources in a holistic and practical manner. Finally, it presents clarifying graphics and exercises that illustrate each of the subsets and the whole in a pragmatic and easily understood format.

WHAT IS IT ABOUT?

This book is about causing systemic high-quality management of change using the subsets of most of the recent restructuring and planning elements that are being tried in school districts. It also lays a knowledge base of information, which assists in making clear why and how all the pieces fit together into a management operating system.

WHAT IS THE STRUCTURE OF THIS BOOK?

The book consists of eleven chapters. The first four chapters lay an informational prerequisite background for the seven chapters to follow.

Chapter 1, "Educational Quality Management and Change: Implications for Schools," relates the considerations decision makers should carefully consider when initiating, reacting to, or managing change of any type.

Chapter 2, "Educational Quality Management and People Theories: Implications for Schools," provides an understanding of a series of important theories that relate to the needs and processes to be considered when dealing with the human elements within schools.

Chapter 3, "Educational Quality Management and Leadership Theories: Implications for Schools," relates a series of theories explaining the various categories of leadership. It emphasizes the roles that leaders can take when leading their schools into new programs and changes.

Chapter 4, "Needs Assessment: A Prerequisite for Achieving Educational Quality Management," discusses the meaning of the word *need* and presents information about micro (subsets of the total—school building, department) needs. It also discusses the methods of identifying large group, small group, and individual needs. Finally, it presents techniques for transforming the identified needs into action programs.

Chapters 5–10 present information about the specific programs and structures that can be integrated into a holistic systemic quality management planning and operations model.

Chapter 5, "Effective Schools Research: Building Blocks for High-Quality Strategic Goals for Schools," presents the basic correlates that have been found to exist in effective schools. It also presents the action planning requirements necessary to implement the effective schools correlates.

Chapter 6, "Outcome-Based Education: Potential Usage as an Educational Quality Management Measurement Delivery System for Schools," relates the advantage of specifying measurable indicators in three levels of results: (1) products, (2) outputs, and (3) outcomes.

Chapter 7, "School-Based Management: An Internal and External Customer Empowerment Structure for Educational Quality Management," describes the structure and processes of School-Based Management (SBM). It also relates the variety of decisions to be made by the building-level decision makers and the central school district–level decision makers and outlines those decisions that are best shared. It presents a case for the development of policies, a method of school-based budgeting, and a method for making personnel decisions. It emphasizes the requirement of extensive training of members of SBM committees.

Chapter 8, "Educational Quality Management Basics: A Systematic Framework for Quality Schools," develops the key characteristics that exist in the quality movement in business and in school districts. It emphasizes the development of customer-related specifications, the goals of quality products and quality services, and the requirement of continuous measurement to assure quality.

Chapter 9, "Establishing Quality Management Strategic and Tactical Plans for Schools," details the required planning steps, which include: (1) arriving at an initial preferred future vision for the schools, (2) developing a guiding mission statement, (3) conducting internal and external scans to determine trendlines that may impact the strategic plans, (4) arriving at a consensus of stakeholders' beliefs and values, (5) determining the Critical Success Factors (CSFs), (6) arriving at a final preferred vision for the schools based upon the information collected in items three through five above, and (7) developing strategic mega (societal), macro (total organization), and micro (subsets of the organization) goals.

Chapter 10, "Combining Total Quality Management, Strategic and Tactical Planning, Effective Schools Research, School-Based Management, and Outcome-Based Measurement into a Holistic Educational Quality Management Change Model: A Powerful Operating System for Schools," emphasizes the integration of all of these subparts into a systematic quality management planning and operating structure and process.

Chapter 11, "Tying It All Together and Projecting the Future of Educational Quality Management in Schools," ends the book by: (1) discussing the advantages of developing an integrated approach to change and restructuring, (2) relating the potential this integrated approach holds for systematic long-term positive change in schools, and (3) envisioning the future of Quality Management in schools.

FOR WHOM IS THIS BOOK WRITTEN?

This book is written for principals, superintendents of schools, board of education members, and all of the stakeholders of school districts who wish to initiate, or who are the recipients of, change in the form of new programs or restructuring thrusts. It is written with the hope that seeing all the pieces of the puzzle as an integrated whole, which utilizes Quality Management as a catalyst for the development of a high-quality systematic planning and operating model, will provide an easily understood and pragmatic tool for those responsible for the quality of the products and services provided by the individual schools and school districts, which have the ultimate responsibility for the education of our most valued resource – the children and youth of this country.

This book will also serve as a valuable resource tool for the professor of education and for graduate students who are learning to become the educational leaders of tomorrow. Finally, it also will serve the purpose for any person who is interested in seeing how all these new restructuring ideas can fit together to improve our schools.

BY WHOM IS THIS BOOK WRITTEN?

This book is written by two very experienced practitioners who have recently decided to spend some of their careers contributing to the graduate education of tomorrow's educational leaders. They have school district–level experiences as teachers at the elementary and secondary levels; as principals, central office administrators, and supervisors; as an assistant superintendent for instruction; and as a long-term superintendent of schools.

In addition, they have served as consultants to numerous school districts in the areas of planning, empowerment, school-based management, and quality management. Also, they have experiences as a state department official, dealing directly with school district assessment, and as a consultant to businesses, universities, national associations, and foundations.

Most importantly, in their own work at the school district level, they utilized varied empowerment structures for teachers, students, administrators, parents, and community members. In addition, they have utilized strategic and tactical planning structures involving thousands of participants, and they have developed Educational Quality Management procedures, which were utilized at both the central district and school-site levels.

JERRY J. HERMAN, PH.D.
JANICE L. HERMAN, PH.D.

CHAPTER 1

Educational Quality Management and Change: Implications for Schools

THIS chapter discusses (1) types of organizational change in which a school or school district might be involved, (2) a vertical change model and its stages, (3) prerequisites for successful management of transformational change, (4) investigation of the school district's or school's readiness for change, (5) characteristics of which the planners and change agents must be aware during the change transition, (6) actions that help ensure that the change will be positive, (7) aids in overcoming resistance to change, (8) stages of an individual's adjustment to change, and (9) enabling behaviors and bridges to new practice.

Educational Quality Management (EQM) requires dramatic change from the traditional management strategies and tactics utilized by schools [1]. Change from the traditional strategy of central control by a board of education and administration is constantly being challenged by those numerous individuals and organizations who feel that our school districts are failing in their mission to produce productive citizens and workers. In its place, such programs as School-Based Management, Effective Schools, Total Quality Management, Outcome-Based Education, Strategic Planning, and Tactical Planning have been introduced into the management techniques of many of the nation's schools [2].

As the transition from traditional management techniques to the more recently introduced management techniques continues, successfully implementing change is the challenge and the quest [3]. Educational Quality Management is about change, and it consolidates a variety of specific management programs into a single transformational change approach.

In 1969, Bennis stated that "change is the biggest story in the world today, and we are not coping with it adequately; change in the size and movement of people; change in the nature, location and availability of jobs; changing relations between students and professors, between workers and employers, between generations, and violent changes at

1

that; violent changes in the cities; . . . and of course, change in the relations between the empires that are falling and the empires that are arising" [4]. These words ring just as true today as they did in 1969. Like a new birth in the family (which provides the opportunity to create a new life's dimensions) and like taxes and death (which provide serious challenges to which one must adjust), change is continuous. We live daily with minor changes; and in our personal lives and in our work lives, we frequently must adjust to major changes. How well, as administrators, teachers, and other school employees, we adjust to changes in our workplace determines how successful we are at doing our jobs; and it, many times, determines the degree of effectiveness, efficiency, and positive environmental work climate that exists in our school buildings and in our school districts [5].

As educational leaders, we are in a dramatic state of flux, and how well we perform the role of change agents may well determine the degree of success that we have in operating our school buildings and school districts. Dramatic cries for change are upon us. Witness the demand for

- student graduates who can make our businesses and industries more competitive in the world's marketplace
- greatly improved performance on standardized achievement test scores
- increased introduction of technology into our teaching stations and into our administrative operations
- greater accountability by all levels of school employees for producing high-quality outcomes
- restructuring, not just modifying, practically everything that happens at our school buildings and school district levels
- choice by students and parents of the school district and/or individual school that the student selects to attend
- School-Based Management, where principals, teachers, and parents (such as that mandated by the Kentucky Reform Act of 1990) are empowered to make numerous budget, instructional, personnel, and governance decisions at the site level
- change! change! change of all structures and processes that exist in our traditional ways of operating our school districts and our individual schools [6]

As educational leaders, it falls upon our shoulders to do out best to adjust to change, but, more importantly, to lead change in the direction we believe it should be headed. We must assume this risk-taking responsibility; for if we can rid ourselves of many of the shackles of the past actions, we can lead our schools to a more productive, effective, efficient, and humane future. McEwan, Carmichael, Short, and Steel pointed out the critical role of leadership and the importance of involving other people in the strategic planning process. They stated "Leadership is the linchpin. Without the exercise of positive leadership at chief executive and board level, effective change does not take place. It is through the will and ability of chief executives and directors that people will become an integral part of the strategic planning process and a source of competitive advantage" [7].

Involving others in the strategic planning process is important because change in education affects everyone: it affects the entire school district, the school buildings, the students, the employees, the policymakers, the facilitators of change, the implementers of change; and it also affects those people who are responsible for planning within the school district. It is clear that everyone involved with a school building's or a school district's operation is somehow involved in the change process.

As we restructure school districts, it is important that we consider and understand the various elements that impact people and organizations when they attempt dramatic change(s). We began this investigation of the various change elements with a discussion of the types of organizational change.

TYPES OF ORGANIZATIONAL CHANGE IN WHICH A SCHOOL OR SCHOOL DISTRICT MIGHT BE INVOLVED

As we determine the requirement to make changes in our educational system, we have initial choices to make. These choices will many times be determined by employee attitudes: community attitudes; desire for change; political pressure from a variety of business, industrial, and governmental sources; and the availability of sufficient resources to assist in making the desired change(s) [8].

The three major procedures for initiating and carrying out change that the district's or school's decision makers have to consider include those of entrepreneurial change, transactional change, and transformational change. Each of these change procedures has advantages when the environment for change is properly assessed by decision makers.

Entrepreneurial change is the preferred change choice when key groups of employees initiate and support the change; but the change is not demanded by the school principal, the school district superintendent, the school board, or some outside source. The success rate of this approach is very high because it has been initiated by and it is owned by those individuals who must initiate, manage, and maintain the change.

Transactional change is a change approach when those decision makers wishing to cause a specific change to take place offer something of equal or greater value to the employees who will cause the change to take place. If the benefit to those who are to initiate, manage, and maintain the desired change is great enough, the probability of success will be very high. If, however, the benefits provided those who will be responsible for making the change work are not sufficient, the change is doomed to a quick death. Such an abortive attempt can also have a long-lasting negative effect on the morale of employees and the effectiveness and efficiency of the school or school district.

Transformational change is the only rational change choice when a school or school district is not working well or when outside or inside forces are demanding radical changes in the way the instructional, governance, and support programs are operating within the school and/or the school district. This category of change is one in which rapid and major structural or process modifications are required for the survival and comfort level within the school organization, within the employees, and within all of the school's or school district's stakeholders [9].

Since transformational change is the most difficult change to successfully implement, the remainder of this discussion will focus on informational items that will assist in making effective and efficient transformational change take place. The first requirement for those who are responsible for initiation of transformational change is that of understanding the various stages of change [10].

A VERTICAL CHANGE MODEL AND ITS STAGES

If the school's or the school district's decision makers are embarking on transformational change, they would be wise to develop a model to guide their change efforts. Of course, before developing their change strategies and tactics, it is clear that they must possess detailed data on the identified needs of the school or the school district. That is, they must identify the future vision of *what should be* or *what could be* (strategic goals defined), and next compare this future vision to the *what is* present state. The discrepancy between the future vision and the present state defines the *needs* to be addressed [11]. The Nine-Stage Vertical Change Model will assist the planners of transformational change to design action programs to meet the identified *needs*, by clearly indicating the stages that must be addressed by the decision makers and the planners as they go about the business of implementing transformational change(s).

NINE-STAGE VERTICAL CHANGE MODEL

START: Status Quo Stage

STEP 1:   Unfreezing (Renewal Stage)

STEP 2:   Awareness of Need Stage (Individual and/or Organization)

STEP 3:   Acceptance of Involvement Stage (Individual)

STEP 4:   Action Planning Stage:
        A. Diagnosing
        B. Exploring alternative solutions
        C. Selecting the "Best Fit" solution
        D. Developing tactical specifications (Who? What? Where? Why? When? and How?)

STEP 5:   Evaluation Stage:
        A. Data collection
        B. Data array
        C. Data analysis

STEP 6:   Decision Stage:
        A. Recycle–Go to any of the previous stages and modify if modifications appear to be required or
        B. Accept the change(s) for implementation within the total organization, and utilize the new structures and processes as Standard Operating Procedures (S.O.P.s).

STEP 7:   Refreezing Stage:
        A. Individuals internalize the change(s).
        B. The organization (school or school district) internalizes the change(s), and they become part of the organizational culture of the school and/or school district.

STEP 8:   Status Quo Reestablished Stage:
The new change structures and processes are purposely maintained and *frozen* into the operational procedures and structures of the school and/or the school district.

STEP 9:   Monitoring Stage:
Determine *needs* (gaps between *what is* and *what should be* or *what could be,* and maintain a readiness state for another unfreezing (renewal) state if one becomes necessary at some future point [12].

PREREQUISITES FOR THE SUCCESSFUL MANAGEMENT OF TRANSFORMATIONAL CHANGE

Once the decision makers have devised a change model, they would do well to review the operational requirements that will enhance the chance of successful management of transformational change; if all of these conditions are not met, those responsible for causing the change to take place will have lessened their chance of success. Lawrie reminds us that "creating, delivering, and evaluating a program of change is a change in itself. Such a program should properly model the principles it is trying to convey" [13]. The prerequisites of such a program include the following:

- commitment to the change by the leadership and key stakeholders
- a clear and written description of the school's or school district's *vision* of *what should be* or *what could be* in the future
- a clear and written description of the *what is* present stage of the school's or school district's operations
- a discrepancy analysis that identifies the *needs* that are indicated when comparing the *what should be* or *what could be* states to the *what is* current state of the school or the school district
- an action plan (with tactics identified) to allow the school or the school district to reach its desired future vision
- training for those individuals who are to plan and/or implement the action plans to achieve the future vision. Indeed, Carnall pointed out that "introducing change in ways that do not encourage learning is likely to entrench negative attitudes to change, in the future. Only if people and organizations change by

learning from the experience of change, can effectiveness be achieved and sustained" [14].
- providing adequate temporal, financial, and human resources to enhance the probability of successfully implementing and operationalizing the desired change(s)
- frequent and high-quality two-way communications throughout the entire change process
- adjustments to be made when called for, even during the process of implementing the desired change(s) (formative changes)
- predicted end results of the change efforts to include achieving the desired outcomes and employees and other stakeholders who are proud of and happy with the change(s) [15]

INVESTIGATING THE SCHOOL DISTRICT'S OR SCHOOL BUILDING'S READINESS FOR CHANGE

Once the decision has been made that transformational change is required, wise leadership determines, as best it can, the readiness change state that both the organization and the individual employees and important stakeholders within the organization currently possess [16]. Figures 1.1 and 1.2 provide questionnaires that will prove helpful in determining the readiness state of both the school or school district and the readiness state of the employees and other important stakeholders of the school or school district.

Once the decision makers or change agents determine the organization's readiness state for change, they should quickly attempt to determine each individual's (employee's or important stakeholder's) readiness for change at the school's or school district's level. Figure 1.2 provides a questionnaire to accomplish this important task.

CHARACTERISTICS OF WHICH THE PLANNERS AND CHANGE AGENTS MUST BE AWARE DURING THE CHANGE TRANSITION

Having assessed the readiness of the school (school district) and the individuals within the school (school district) for change and having developed a strategic and tactical planning change model, the local decision makers would do well to put in place actions that will help

DIRECTIONS: circle the number which most clearly identifies your attitude toward the statements listed.

Strongly Agree (4)	Agree (3)	Disagree (2)	Strongly Disagree (1)
1. My school (school district) has a clear *vision* of *what should be* and *what could be* in the future.	4	3	2	1
2. My school (school district) has a clear picture of *what is* currently in existence.	4	3	2	1
3. My school (school district) has a clear idea of the *needs* (differences or *gaps* between *what is* and *what should be* in the future) which should be addressed.	4	3	2	1
4. Outside forces are requiring my school (school district) to make transformational change(s).	4	3	2	1
5. Internal forces are requiring my school (school district) to make transformational change(s).	4	3	2	1
6. My school (school district) is constantly looking for ways to improve its structures and/or processes.	4	3	2	1
7. My school (school district) is constantly encouraging us to present new ideas to improve ourselves and our school (school district).	4	3	2	1
8. My school (school district) promotes continuous and accurate communication with all employees and all stakeholders.	4	3	2	1
9. My school (school district) invests a considerable amount of funds in staff development and training activities for all categories of employees.	4	3	2	1
10. My school (school district) collects data on results and determines the impacts of our efforts.	4	3	2	1
11. If we try something new at my school (in my school district) and it doesn't work well, my principal (superintendent or board of education) does not hold it against us.	4	3	2	1
12. My school principal (superintendent or board of education) gives everyone credit for successes achieved.	4	3	2	1

Figure 1.1. An organization's change readiness questionnaire.

DIRECTIONS: circle the number which most clearly identifies your attitude toward the statements listed.

Strongly Agree (4)	Agree (3)	Disagree (2)		Strongly Disagree (1)
13. My school (school district) publicly celebrates every success and every milestone attained.	4	3	2	1
14. My school (school district) looks towards the future with its visioning, lays immediate and continuous plans to achieve its preferred future vision, and uses the past and current accomplishments as baselines upon which to improve.	4	3	2	1
TOTAL READINESS SCORE:				

Figure 1.1 (continued). An organization's change readiness questionnaire.

ensure that the desired change(s) will become positive ones. This preparedness involves: (1) understanding the characteristics that exist during the transitional period of change, (2) actions that will help ensure that the change(s) is (are) positive in nature, and (3) helping others to overcome their resistance to change [17].

During the various stages of development towards a change, the planners of change and the local decision makers must realize that the following characteristics exist:

- Past patterns of behavior are highly valued, and they are not easily given up by individuals or organizations.
- Emotional stress usually exists in many individuals and in many areas of the organization. The ultimate future is unknown, and many times those structures and processes that are to remain stable are not clarified.
- Much energy is wasted because of resistance to change or because of uncertainty about the future role of the individual or of the structure of the organization and processes that the organization will utilize. Also, rumors often run rampant during the transitional stages of change(s).
- Often, negative conflicts will arise during the transitional periods.
- Sometimes organized opposition will arise in an attempt to block the change(s) [18].

DIRECTIONS: please circle the number which most clearly identifies your attitude.			
Strongly Agree (4)	Agree (3)	Disagree (2)	Strongly Disagree (1)

1. I have a clear vision of what my school (school district) should be like in the future.	4	3	2	1
2. I have a clear *vision* of what my school (school district) should be like in the future.	4	3	2	1
3. When comparing the future and the present, I can identify *needs* (gaps between *what is* and *what should be* or *could be*) which we can address to improve my school (school district).	4	3	2	1
4. I realize external forces will cause me to change.	4	3	2	1
5. I realize internal forces will cause me to change.	4	3	2	1
6. I enjoy new challenges and new ways of doing things.	4	3	2	1
7. I am constantly trying to improve myself and to improve what I am doing.	4	3	2	1
8. I enjoy receiving recognition for making positive changes.	4	3	2	1
9. If I am unsuccessful in my change efforts, I am determined to keep trying until I succeed.	4	3	2	1
10. I look forward to taking part in new learning opportunities through staff development and training programs.	4	3	2	1
11. I take time to celebrate my making successful changes and reaching desired milestones.	4	3	2	1
12. I look towards the future, I plan for the present, and I use the past and the present as baselines upon which to improve.	4	3	2	1
TOTAL READINESS SCORE:				_____

Figure 1.2. An individual's change readiness questionnaire.

ACTIONS THAT HELP ENSURE THAT THE CHANGE(S) WILL BE POSITIVE

Principals, superintendents, boards of education, change agents, and planners can take many steps that will lessen the degree of resistance to change(s). Carnall reminds us that "by definition change upsets the 'status quo.' Leadership is central because achieving effective organizational change requires us to elevate analysis over consensus. Easy options are in short supply" [19]. As a result, leaders should provide detailed information about what will be changed and what will remain as it always has operated. They should provide security statements to the individuals who will be expected to initiate and maintain the desired changes. Finally, they should assure the individuals involved that they will be important sources of information about the best methods of changing the structures and processes used by the school or the school district [20].

They should communicate the expected positive benefits of the contemplated change(s), they should commit adequate resources to ensure a successful change strategy, and they should honor the past accomplishments of individuals and the organization (school or school district) while transitioning to the desired future state. They should also plan thoroughly, monitor consistently, assess potential and actual impacts as the transition evolves, and evaluate the level of outcomes achieved when compared to the desired outcomes of the change.

In addition, they should plan rewards and recognition for those individuals who assist in planning and implementing the change; they should provide visible celebrations as each change milestone is reached. Tregoe and Tobia reinforced this point when they stated that "all the talk about strategy is not enough to keep everyone strategically focused. Day-to-day pressure is too intense and can easily overwhelm strategy; incentives sustain momentum" [21]. They should have previously developed contingency plans to deal with the logical, emotional, individual, and group forms of resistance to change. Finally, they should involve everyone in a major celebration when the desired change(s) is (are) completed.

AIDS IN OVERCOMING RESISTANCE TO CHANGE

To help ensure that the change(s) enacted will be positive, there are many things that change agents, planners, and local decision makers can do. Below is a list of factors that assist in causing positive change to be accomplished.

A Baker's Dozen of Factors That Assist in Causing Positive Organizational (School or School District) Change

(1) The current state has been unfrozen due to a singular reason or a combination of reasons.

(2) Key people in the school or school district investigate change or are required to make change due to forceful variables that impact the organization.

(3) A critical mass of stakeholders inside and/or outside the school desire, or at least permit, change to take place.

(4) A *vision* of *what should be* or *what could be* exists, at least among key people in the school or the school district.

(5) These same key people must possess a clear view of the *what is* state of the school or the school district.

(6) The key people must reach a consensus on the discrepancies (gaps) between the future vision and the present state that defines the *needs* that must be met and for which action programs must be planned.

(7) Based upon these identified needs, strategic goals and specific objectives must be determined.

(8) Action programs and tactical plans must be developed with the goal of achieving the identified strategic goals and objectives.

(9) Training of those persons who are to initiate and maintain the change(s) must take place, and the appropriate amount of resources must be allocated for training of the participants in such areas as:
  • developing communications skills
  • learning planning techniques
  • implementing strategies and tactics
  • conducting impact studies
  • evaluating the results of the action plans

(10) Communication systems must be devised for use throughout the change stages of planning, implementing, and evaluating; and the communications must be two-way, comprehensive, open, truthful, and accurate.

(11) Ownership must exist by at least a critical mass of all stakeholders of the school or the school district.

(12) Continuous attention must be paid to the needs of individuals and the organization during the planning and implementing phases of the change(s) since the individuals' needs are at least as important, if not more important, than the organization's needs if the change efforts are to be successful [22].

(13) Once the desired change(s) is (are) accomplished, individuals feel ownership of the change(s), and the change(s) has (have) become part of the organization's ongoing culture; it is crucial that the refreezing of this change state takes place. If this does not happen, unplanned and undesired changes will continue to surface.

Up to this point the focus has been primarily on the organization and what will assist the organization (school and/or school district) to make positive change(s). At this point, the focus most clearly turns to the individuals who are to enact and carry out the desired change(s).

STAGE OF AN INDIVIDUAL'S ADJUSTMENT TO CHANGE

Most individuals are not immediately comfortable with change. In fact, as is true in their personal lives, they go through adjustment stages when their organization (school or school district) is in a change state [23]. Most individuals, when involved in forced organizational change, will go through stages similar to those listed below. Some individuals may begin at higher change acceptance stages than others, and some individuals may skip or combine a stage or two; but most will go through these eight stages in the sequence presented:

- stage one: denial
- stage two: defensiveness
- stage three: interest
- stage four: involvement
- stage five: acceptance
- stage six: adaptation
- stage seven: internalization
- stage eight: ownership

To understand why individuals go through these various stages before they accept ownership of the desired change(s), all that is required is to think about some of the defensive reasons individuals offer for not making the change(s). This is important, as Veninga pointed out by stating that "no matter how carefully you have diagnosed an organization's health, and no matter how precisely you defined the targets of change, resistance is likely. Therefore, for any program to be successful, it is imperative that the reasons for resistance be identified, studied, and addressed" [24]. Although additional reasons for resistance to change could be listed, many of the common ones are

- "It was tried before, and it wasn't successful."
- "It costs too much to make this change."
- "It's not my job."
- "It's never been done before."
- "It's impractical."
- "Let's not rush into anything."
- "We've always done it this way."
- "It's impossible to do."
- "I don't have the time."
- "I'm already overworked."
- "It won't work."
- "It's too far into the future."
- "I (we) will lose control."
- "I don't want any surprises."
- "New things will cause me to do more work."

If the planners and decision makers will put themselves in the shoes of those individuals whom they will be asking to implement and maintain the desired change(s), they will be better able to anticipate the actions that will have to be taken to counteract negative attitudes and change resistance. Figure 1.3 presents a series of questions that will serve this purpose for planners and decision makers at the school and the school district levels.

Now that we have investigated the various stages of change and the planning that must take place to enhance the probability of enacting positive change(s), we turn to those behaviors that serve as enablers of change(s).

ENABLING BEHAVIORS AND BRIDGES TO NEW PRACTICE

The dramatic change demanded by the implementation of EQM implies a substantive change in the attitudes and perceptions of the school

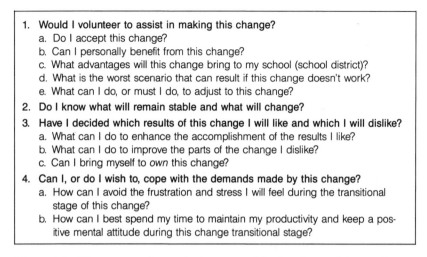

1. Would I volunteer to assist in making this change?
   a. Do I accept this change?
   b. Can I personally benefit from this change?
   c. What advantages will this change bring to my school (school district)?
   d. What is the worst scenario that can result if this change doesn't work?
   e. What can I do, or must I do, to adjust to this change?
2. Do I know what will remain stable and what will change?
3. Have I decided which results of this change I will like and which I will dislike?
   a. What can I do to enhance the accomplishment of the results I like?
   b. What can I do to improve the parts of the change I dislike?
   c. Can I bring myself to *own* this change?
4. Can I, or do I wish to, cope with the demands made by this change?
   a. How can I avoid the frustration and stress I will feel during the transitional stage of this change?
   b. How can I best spend my time to maintain my productivity and keep a positive mental attitude during this change transitional stage?

Figure 1.3. Change questions: placing yourself in the shoes of those who are asked or forced to implement and maintain the change(s).

district participants [25]. Groups of stakeholders will have justifiable reasons for resisting the wholesale change implied in EQM. The typical history of organizational "bombardment" with change and the concerns for lack of time, money, energy, motivation, and personal return on the investment create a mass of disincentives for the contemplation of significant change. It is critical, therefore, that the assurances described in the section on actions aimed at ensuring positive change are directed at such key groups as employee organizations and school boards [26].

For a more focused effort, there are many formal training packages and programs that are intended to facilitate change in schools. It would be wise, if there is a substantive level of unwillingness or unreadiness to change, to implement such training in order to lay the groundwork for systemic alteration and dramatic work environment change. Following this preparation, such EQM-themed informational avenues as retreats, workshops, and dissemination of written and electronic updates on the quality concept could be used.

SUMMARY

This chapter has presented the substantive changes required by Educational Quality Management implementation, as they fit into the context of the challenge such a transformational process presents. Examples of change as an environmental constant, particularly in the fluctuating education field, were given. The role of educators in leading and facilitating change was discussed.

The types of organizational change that might be required in a school district include entrepreneurial, transactional, and transformational change. The connections between transformational change and the strategic planning process were explored through the description and presentation of a vertical change model. The prerequisites for the successful management of transformational change were listed, including commitment, clarity of the present state and identified needs, the development of an action plan, training and resources, communication, ongoing adjustments, and the attainment of desired outcomes. Questionnaires to determine an organization's and an individual's change readiness were provided.

Particular characteristics of these change processes were identified; leadership actions that help ensure positive changes were described. A list of strategies that assist positive organizational change was also provided. Also included was a description of an individual's normal reactions to change and a series of questions aimed at sensing and coping with the responses.

REFERENCES

1. Conner, D. and S. Hughes. 1988. "Architects of the Future—Managing Change," *CUPA Journal*, 39(4):15–18.
2. Kaufman, R., J. J. Herman and K. Watters. Forthcoming. *Planning Educational Systems: What, When, How.* Lancaster, PA: Technomic Publishing Company, Inc.
3. Carnall, C. 1986. "Managing Strategic Change: An Integrated Approach," *Long Range Planning,* 19(6):105–115.
4. Bennis, W. 1969. *Organizational Development: Its Nature, Origins and Prospects.* Reading, MA: Addison-Wesley Publishing Company, p. 2.
5. Lawrie, J. 1990. "The ABS'c of Change Management," *Training and Development Journal,* 44(3):87–89.
6. Howlett, P. 1987. "Issue Management: Passing Fad or Ultimate Solution?" *Thrust for Educational Leadership,* 6(4):8–10.
7. McEwen, N., C. Carmichael, D. Short and A. Steel. 1988. "Managing Organizational Change—A Strategic Approach," *Long Range Planning,* 21(6):71–78.
8. Case, T., R. Vandenberg and P. Meredith. 1990. "Internal and External Change Agents," *Leadership and Organization Development Journal,* 11(1):4–15.
9. Herman, J. J. and J. L. Herman. In press. *Making Change Happen.* Newbury Park, CA: Corwin Press, a Sage Publications Company.

10. Gummer, B. 1990. "Managing Organizational Cultures: Management Science or Management Ideology?" *Administration in Social Work,* 14(1):135–153.
11. Kaufman, R. and J. J. Herman. 1991. *Strategic Planning in Education.* Lancaster, PA: Technomic Publishing Company, Inc., pp. 89–108.
12. Herman, J. J. 1988. "Map the Trip to Your District's Future," *The School Administrator,* 45(9):16, 18, 23.
13. Lawrie, p. 89.
14. Carnall, p. 114.
15. Herman, J. J. and J. L. Herman. 1991. *The Positive Development of Human Resources and School District Organizations.* Lancaster, PA: Technomic Publishing Company, Inc., pp. 52–68.
16. Leonard-Barton, D. 1988. "Implementation Characteristics of Organizational Innovations," *Communication Research,* 15(5):603–631.
17. Harvey, T. 1990. *Checklist for Change: A Pragmatic Approach to Creating and Controlling Change.* Boston, MA: Allyn and Bacon.
18. Kanter, R. 1987. "Managing Traumatic Change: Avoiding the 'Unlucky 13,' " *Management Review,* 76(5):23–24.
19. Carnall, p. 105.
20. Wiener, Y. 1988. "Forms of Value Systems: A Focus on Organizational Effectiveness and Cultural Change and Maintenance," *Academy of Management Review,* 13(4):534–545.
21. Tregoe, B. and P. Tobia. 1990. "An Action-Oriented Approach to Strategy," *The Journal of Business Strategy,* 1(1):16–21.
22. Herman, J. J. and J. L. Herman. 1993. *School Based Management: Current Thinking and Practice.* Springfield, IL: Charles C. Thomas, Publishers, pp. 30–34.
23. Kilmann, R. 1985. "Managing All Barriers to Organizational Success," *Training and Development Journal,* 39(9):64–72.
24. Veninga, R. 1987. "In Search of Excellence: Practical Strategies for Managing Change in Environmental Health," *Journal of Environmental Health,* 50(1):4–7.
25. Herman, J. J. 1993. "Total Quality Management," *Educational Facilities Planner,* 31(1):30.
26. Patterson, J. L. 1993. *Leadership for Tomorrow's Schools.* Alexandria, VA: Association for Supervision and Curriculum Development, pp. 42–43.

CHAPTER 2

Educational Quality Management and People Theories: Implications for Schools

THIS chapter focuses on the classic human behavioral models and concepts that provide an understanding of a series of important theories that relate to the needs and processes to be considered when dealing with the human elements within schools. These informational prerequisites will underpin the behavioral assumptions upon which Total Quality Management (TQM) is based. The nature of motivation—both individual and collective—lies at the heart of TQM; therefore, a sense of the dynamics of the basic components that activate, direct, and sustain human behavior is essential to understanding educational quality. The elements to be considered in this chapter include: (1) Maslow's Hierarchy of Needs theory, (2) McGregor's Theory X & Y, (3) Ouchi's Theory Z, (4) Herzberg's Hygiene/Motivator theory, and (5) enabling behaviors and bridges to new practice.

PRIMARY CONSIDERATIONS ABOUT PEOPLE AND MOTIVATION

Motivation, in general, can be considered as a process governing individual choices among differing forms of voluntary activities. A number of other concepts, such as drive, need, incentive, reward, reinforcement, expectancy, and goal setting, are frequently included in the consideration of motivation. It can be more succinctly defined as "the complex forces, drives, needs, tension states, or other mechanisms that start and maintain voluntary activity toward the achievement of personal goals" [1].

MASLOW'S HIERARCHY OF NEEDS THEORY

Five basic needs comprise the Maslovian model, and they are interrelated and arranged in a hierarchy of ascending importance. The first level is physiological—the basic biological needs of each individual. The second level is that of safety and security, including freedom from danger of personal and societal threat. The need for an orderly social and legal structure is included here. The third level is that of belonging, love, and social activities; this need has been linked to dysfunction in youth and is a critical need in contemporary society. The relatedness represents a kind of psychological survival [2]. The fourth level is concerned with esteem: the need for self-respect and for the respect of others. Such qualities as strength, achievement, adequacy, mastery, competence, independence, and freedom have been connected with this need. Also connected have been the qualities of reputation/prestige, status, dominance, recognition, appreciation, importance, and attention. The fifth level need, self-actualization, is concerned with the desire for self-fulfillment, the need to be what an individual wants to be, achieving and maximizing the potential of the individual's capacities and competencies. The hierarchical arrangement of the needs reflects a developmental process; the successive emergence of higher level needs is dependent on some level of satisfaction of the preceding needs. Likewise, the theory includes the assumption that when self-actualization occurs, the entire hierarchy is strengthened [3,4].

There are clear connections between the higher Maslovian levels of need and the outcomes and advantages of a quality-driven system of management. Ishikawa [5] described them as:

- experiencing the satisfaction that comes from being able to utilize one's own abilities to the fullest and from growing as a person
- having self-confidence, and becoming a self-fulfilled person
- using one's own brain, working voluntarily, and, in this way, contributing to society

Maslow has argued that, for most workers, the first three levels of need are normally satisfied and are therefore no longer motivational in nature; however, satisfaction of esteem and self-actualization are seldom completed and will therefore serve as continual motivators [6]. The implication for educational organizations is that methods must be developed to satisfy more fully the high level needs of students, teachers, and administrators.

McGREGOR'S THEORY X AND Y

This more behavioral type of motivational theory is based on philosophical assumptions about beliefs about human nature. McGregor's

Theory X, primarily a negativistic view, includes assumptions held by supervisors and management about people's inherent lack of motivation. It views people as instinctively disliking and avoiding work and stresses the need to apply coercion, strong direction, or threat of some kind of consequence in order to have them work towards organizational goals or outcomes. There is an assumption that workers, essentially ambitionless, desire direction and an absence of responsibility. The implication is that only the lower Maslovian levels of need are truly motivational.

His Theory Y, by contrast, has a more positive view of human motivation, in its view of the natural instinct and desire for both mental and physical work. In the attainment of organizational goals, workers will employ self-direction and self-control if they feel commitment to the objectives; and that commitment is associated with the achievement of goals. Individuals instinctively seek and accept responsibility and will apply creativity, ingenuity, and imagination toward solving organizational concerns. These fundamental assumptions about the basic nature of human beings directly impacts relationships to work and to organizational life.

Certainly, the externally controlled, traditional managerial approaches of the early part of this century have been more Theory X in nature, with regard to management's beliefs about the nature of people. The key to the more self-controlled Theory Y beliefs is that they reflect what is inherent in the individual worker and that it is the very nature of the tightly controlled organization that causes the need for external control; the experience of most workers has not tapped the motivational resources available. Worker commitment to and involvement with organizational objectives, under proper conditions, will result in the more fluid and consensus-driven type of managerial style suggested by Theory Y [7,8].

Obviously, the Total Quality elements of utilizing one's own abilities in a voluntary way to support organizational goals and the sense of common commitment to those goals create a match between McGregor's Theory Y and the prerequisites for quality management.

OUCHI'S THEORY Z

In reviewing Japanese and American businesses, William Ouchi proposed that the notable successes in both environments were functions of a distinctive corporate culture, which was very internally consistent and which was characterized by the shared values of intimacy, trust, cooperation, teamwork, and egalitarianism. The critical role of management was in the successful use of human resources, the effective management of people, rather than in any technological advantage. These Theory Z organizational cultures have distinctive hallmarks: employment security, which results in long-term personal investment in the organization; more opportunities for broadening experiences and diverse career paths through slower promotion rates; participative and shared-consensus decision making, which requires cooperation, teamwork, common values, and mutual trust; and concern for the whole employee [9,10].

These organization possess Total Quality elements in the common culture of shared core values and in the push for attainment of common goals. The holistic design and orientation of these organizations is client service–driven and, in that sense, facilitates the quality dynamics described previously.

HERZBERG'S HYGIENE/MOTIVATOR THEORY

This content theory of motivation has as its basic premise that one set of rewards contributes to job satisfaction and a separate set to job dissatisfaction. The distinction is made by terming the factors that contribute only to minimal job satisfaction *hygienes;* these include such factors as interpersonal relations, policy and administration, technical supervision, and working conditions. They are unique in that their absence contributes to negative worker attitudes and job dissatisfaction. Their mere presence is insufficient to insure genuine motivation or satisfaction with the job; it simply prevents dissatisfaction. Those factors identified as *motivators,* including achievement, recognition, the work/task itself, responsibility, and advancement increase job satisfaction—a distinct dimension of a person's attitude about work, entirely different from hygienes. For maximum worker motivation, both sets of factors must be present. The total elements in the motivating factors are interrelated; they represent the basic needs of personal growth and motivation described in the other theories and have implications for work design and for organizational structure [11,12].

Any attempts, therefore, to use job design for employee motivation must first ensure that dissatisfaction with the hygiene factors are minimized. The work design can be effectively altered to allow employees to experience the motivators. Those job characteristics that might be changed to allow for such motivation to occur might be skill variety, task identity, task significance, autonomy, and feedback. Skill variety involves the array of tasks and talents that are demanded by the job. In task identity, the degree to which the job requires completion and a visible outcome is the focus, as opposed to a job with more disconnected and repetitious tasks. Related to this is task significance, which is the degree to which a job has a substantial impact on the lives or work of other people. Autonomy is the degree to which the job requires substantial freedom and independence, and feedback refers to the degree to which the execution of the work results in the individual obtaining meaningful information about performance effectiveness. Through such change, the work experience is altered, leading to such outcomes as higher internal motivation, higher quality work performance, improved satisfaction with the work, and a lower rate of absenteeism and employee turnover [13].

Again, the basic structure of TQM is a close match for this motivational theory in the focus on performance, on individual contribution and continuous improvement, and on the enlargement and enrichment of worker tasks to enhance the view of the organization as a holistic system.

ENABLING BEHAVIORS AND BRIDGES TO NEW PRACTICE

The theories and models described in this chapter are intended to provide a conceptual framework for the chapters to follow and to point out the behavioral and motivational underpinnings of TQM. The theories are obviously interrelated and logically support the quality concepts that will be expanded upon in later chapters.

Summarily, if employees feel that (1) they are doing meaningful work, (2) they are recognized for their contributions, (3) they have opportunities for input into decisions affecting them, (4) they have security, (5) they are socially accepted, and (6) they have growth opportunities, they will want to improve their performance and the performance of the entire school district. They will be willing to help others and to support the school district in whatever way they can, to contribute to that improvement goal—to function, essentially, as a *quality* organization.

Certain philosophies of management underlie business practices in schools, as in other organizations. Contrary to traditional theories about human behavior and motivation, in contemporary managerial theory, workers are seen as capable of self-directed effort toward shared organizational goals. The primary challenge of management is one of organizing the enterprise in such a way that the potential for self-directed activities, even for innovation, can be tapped.

To do so will require, in many school districts, a profound cultural change and a significant alteration in the existing organizational structure [14,15]. Most school districts are designed for the traditional type of management and supervision, both in hierarchical design and in policy and practice. Staff development and retraining must be aimed at reconceptualizing both the workplace and the employee as an integral and contributing part of the overall organizational structure. Employing contemporary motivational theory and practice as the primary and organizing focus in human resource management will be a long-term undertaking, one that will seek to fuel the quality concept with total employee potential and energy.

SUMMARY

This chapter outlined classic theories of behavioral models and concepts dealing with the human elements within schools. These theories are prerequisites for Total Quality Management. One of the elements considered was Maslow's Hierarchy of Needs theory, a classic structure, which is built around ascending levels of human physical, social, psychological, and emotional needs, and which culminates in self-actualization and self-esteem. McGregor's Theories X and Y are framed around contrasting views of manager-worker and worker-task relationships. The traditional X model emphasizes the need for close supervision and a more punitive system of management, based on the assumption of a human aversion to work. Theory Y is based on beliefs about the inherent human instinct and desire for both mental and physical work. In the attainment of organizational goals, workers will employ self-direction and self-control if they feel responsibility and commitment to the objectives.

Ouchi's Theory Z proposes that the notable successes in business are functions of a distinctive corporate culture, which is very internally consistent and which was characterized by the shared values of intimacy, trust, cooperation, teamwork, and egalitarianism.

Herzberg's Hygiene/Motivator theory describes motivation as having one set of rewards, which contributes to job satisfaction, and a separate set, which contributes to job dissatisfaction. Hygienes—interpersonal relations, policy and administration, technical supervision, and working conditions—are unique in that their absence contributes to negative worker attitudes and job dissatisfaction. Factors identified as motivators—achievement, recognition, the work/task itself, responsibility, and advancement—increase job satisfaction. This distinction between the two dimensions of motivation is significant. The chapter ended with a perspective of the cultural and organizational changes implied by the motivational and behavioral theories that are prerequisite for the implementation of educational quality management.

REFERENCES

1. Hoy, W. K. and C. G. Miskel. 1987. *Educational Administration, Third Edition.* New York, NY: Random House, p. 176.
2. Hampton, D. R., C. E. Summer and R. A. Webber. 1987. *Organizational Behavior and the Practice of Management.* Glenview, IL: Scott, Foresman and Company, p. 44.
3. Ibid., pp. 44–52.
4. Hoy and Miskel, pp. 178–182.
5. Ishikawa, K. As cited in Bonstingl, J. J. 1992. *Schools of Quality: An Introduction to Total Quality Management in Education.* Alexandria, VA: Association for Supervision and Curriculum Development, p. 17.
6. Hampton, Summer and Webber, pp. 179–180.
7. Ibid., pp. 43–44.
8. Rush, H. M. F. 1987. "The Behavioral Sciences," in *Training and Development Handbook, Third Edition,* Robert L. Craig (ed.), New York, NY: McGraw-Hill, pp. 135–167.
9. Hoy and Miskel, pp. 250–251.
10. Herman, J. J. 1992. "Key Steps to Develop School Governance Teams," *The School Administrator,* 49(1):34–35.
11. Herman, J. J. 1989. "Strategic Planning—One of the Changing Leadership Roles of the Principal," *The Clearing House,* 63(2):56–58.
12. Ibid., pp. 9–11.
13. Rush, pp. 146–147.
14. Herman, J. J. and J. L. Herman. 1991. *The Positive Development of Human Resources and School District Organizations.* Lancaster, PA: Technomic Publishing Company, Inc., pp. 19–20.
15. Herman, J. J. and J. L. Herman. In press. *Making Change Happen.* Newbury Park, CA: Corwin Press, a Sage Publications Company.

CHAPTER 3

Educational Quality Management and Leadership Theories: Implications for Schools

THIS chapter presents (1) the basic concepts related to the leadership theories of traits and characteristics of leaders, (2) the analysis of leaders' power and influence, (3) behavioral approaches, (4) the identification of situational factors that affect leaders, (5) the more current transactional and transformational models, and (6) enabling behaviors and bridges to new practice.

The relationship of leadership to educational quality is implied in early quality management theory. The first pioneer in the field of quality, W. Edwards Deming, describes a permanent need for management to "create constancy of purpose for the improvement of product and service." It is the responsibility of management, through appropriate leadership, to create the environment under which quality processes take place [1].

EARLY TRAIT THEORIES

Historical approaches (during the late nineteenth and early twentieth centuries) on leadership were focused on the identification of personal traits, skills, and characteristics that distinguish leaders from nonleaders, or effective leaders from ineffective leaders. These early notions ascribed success to the possession of extraordinary abilities, such as insight and intuition. These theories were later considered inadequate, lacking situational context and flexible application across many managerial environments. However, these early formula-driven findings did reveal some leadership traits and skills that can be considered as germane to and supportive of Total Quality Management. The early research [2–4] shows that effective leaders tend to:

- be more concerned with achieving results than with conforming to policy and procedure; to be more practical than philosophical

- exceed follower ratings on such dimensions as self-confidence, maturity, persistence, and frustration/stress tolerance
- be highly motivated, with strong needs for achievement and power
- be more willing to confront people constructively on work-related issues
- have higher levels of managerial competence in conceptual, technical, and human relations skills
- be more interested in the work task itself than in such matters as compensation and working conditions
- communicate with others openly and honestly
- be more likely to encourage participation of followers in planning, problem solving, and decision making
- maintain a balance between a task orientation and a people orientation
- identify with superiors and with the organization

The thrust of leadership in a quality-oriented organization is toward the creation of an appropriate environment for the systemwide conditions under which quality processes take place. The attitudes and behaviors implied in the leadership trait findings point toward the enhancement of such an environment, where a holistic view of the organization is critical and where the skillful management and maximization of human resources is the key to quality and success.

POWER AND INFLUENCE APPROACH

Another major line of leadership theory is concerned with the source and amount of power and the way in which leaders use power. Influencing the activities of others is fundamental to the exercise of leadership [5]. In a broad sense, a leader's potential to influence others in an organizational context is described in two terms: *position power* and *personal power.* Position power is the formal authority vested in the leader's office; the position itself carries weight, regardless of its occupant. Rank, reward systems, and status are involved in this type of power; it is more often seen in the distribution of rewards, the threat of punishment, and the influence through the conferral of authority "rights," such as that employed in military organizations. By contrast, personal power is the potential influence stemming from the characteristics of the person in the office. Key findings [6,7] about leadership and personal power have revealed that:

- Leader-follower influence processes are reciprocal; both sides mutually shape their behaviors.
- Effective leaders rely more on personal rather than positional power, though a balance between both is needed.
- The manner in which power is used is critical to the result—the outcome of the attempt to use power.
- Effective leaders use power more subtly, maintaining a sensitivity to the feelings of followers.
- When power is used to inspire and encourage rather than dominate followers, it is more productive for the organization and for the individual follower.
- True charismatic leaders tend to use a combination of both positive and negative styles as they employ power.

Again, the wholistic view of the organization and the dependency on the full participation and commitment of followers, in a supportive and nurturing environment, is critical to the implementation of Quality Management.

BEHAVIORAL APPROACH

This approach focuses more on what effective leaders *do,* rather than what they should *be.* During the 1950s, studies at Ohio State University and at the University of Michigan evolved concepts regarding the two dimensions of task/work orientation, known as "initiating structure," and the interactive "consideration" for people. Other theorists, such as Tannenbaum and Schmidt in 1973, have derived a theory of seven leader (manager) types and created a continuum of *manager concern* versus *worker concern.* Blake and Mouton's 1964 classic *Managerial Grid* model reveals a combination of task concern and people concern, describing such combinations as: an insensitive manager high on task but low on people, an abdicating manager low on both, a "country club" manager high on people but low on task, and a middle-of-the-road manager. Their ideal was the leader high on both dimensions [8].

These two-dimensional leaders, capable of paying attention to administrative tasks but simultaneously attending to the follower's need for consideration, support, and trust, possess "quality-friendly" characteristics, such as [9]:

- the ability to increase follower commitment by involving subordinates in appropriate decisions and projects
- the inclination to establish clear performance objectives for subordinates and to treat them with respect and support
- the use of praise and recognition to motivate all types of followers, as well as the use of other incentives
- the use of both consideration and initiating structure to improve group performance
- the ability to have a flexible outlook and to function in changing and uncertain situations

SITUATIONAL APPROACH

Earlier leadership theories were more simplistic; their inadequacy in empirical data led to the extension of the combination with group effectiveness in the *contingency* concept model. As static concepts, trait and behavioral models require the dynamic of some situational application. Consideration of possessed characteristics and the observations of how leaders made things happen was lacking the dimension of environment and behaviorially specific description.

Situationality, or contingency, then, emerged as a leadership theory that maintains that neither traits nor behavior are as important as the factors operating in any given situation. Such variables as the nature of the task, the authority of the leader, and the role expectations of the players – leaders, colleagues, and subordinates – impinge on the situation and require a more specific and tailored leadership response. One such model is Fiedler's 1950s situational theory, which proposed that there was one best leadership trait (style) for a situation and that, optimally, a match of leader to situation should be made. Barring that, the situation should be altered to fit the manager, since it is easier to change circumstances than inherent traits.

Vroom and Yetton's 1973 decision-making model is a highly contingent process that maps decision routes via a decision tree with consideration given for the required quality of the pending decision, the level of acceptance required by followers, and the factor of time for the process to take place in light of the urgency of the decision. Another model considers three variables interacting upon each other in the more complex contingency approach of interaction between situation, leader behavior, and follower response. House's 1974 Path-Goal theory has eight possible combinations in its consideration of leader behaviors (directive, achievement-oriented, supportive, and participative), acted upon and acting upon situationality needs and follower goals. The 1977 Hersey Blanchard model of follower maturity level combined with situationality calls for a repertoire of skills from the leader as the task situation changes over their model's four quadrants. This approach considers the developmental readiness of the follower as related to the task; a new employee requires much directive leadership due to lack of information and expertise; the second quadrant addresses the somewhat experienced but still uniformed employee requiring motivation ("selling or coaching"). As expertise develops further but interpersonal relationships cause difficulty, the third quadrant of the model applies supportive leadership. Expertise combined with intrinsic motivation in the fourth quadrant evokes delegating behaviors from the leader, in an emancipatory and empowering sense. Contingency, then, is a highly significant approach that is more complex to assess in the added dimensions involved; the theory always is expressed in models often more comprehensive than were the earlier ones [10].

The connections with Quality Management are again clear; the need for consideration and inclusion of multiple situationalities in the exercise of leadership speaks to the need for a quality organization's focus on continuous improvement. Similarly, the removal of barriers to facilitate frontline workers and the obtaining of necessary resources for ongoing training, which are part of the leadership role in Quality Management, are situationally driven requirements.

TRANSACTIONAL AND TRANSFORMATIONAL LEADERSHIP

More complex style leadership theorists appeared during the late 1970s and 1980s, with the added dimensions of leader behavior crossed with follower response; the resultant interactions produced a fluent and richly detailed set of theories.

The *transactional* model of leadership is more closely related to situational leadership; it is the capacity to blend, in a situationally responsive manner, the leader responses to subordinate expectation and the demands of the organizational task, frequently making tradeoffs and exchanges between the two in order to maintain that balance [11,12]. Of more contemporary and field-applicable significance is the concept of *transformational leadership*. These types of leaders display a significant variety of leadership styles; their most commonly definable theme, however, is one of leader vision and logic [13,14]. Such logic—combining that far-seeing vision with a solid knowledge base of organizational fact—is characterized by logic that is gestalt in nature, holistic, creative, innovative, and transformative. Transformational leaders envision the entire organization, the complexities of its environment, and its internal and external structure as one entity.

Bass's research in 1981, for example, contains two transactional components (contingent reinforcement and leadership by exception). Other transformational components—charisma orientation, concern for others, and intellectual stimulation—have been found in other models. Similarly, McBer's 1974 components of control, consideration, reward, reinforcement, motivation, standards, and trust are similar in concept to Bass's components. Pulitzer Prize–winning Burns's 1978 book on leadership described the contemporary process of *transactional* to *transformational* style, a developmental step beyond the previous exchange of compliance for some reinforcement system that characterized the transactional dimension. At that stage, there was not an attempt to engage the follower in anything but a brokerage relationship; there was no uplift or inspiration provided. In Bennis' research on the reputational CEOs, the four components—again an echo of the previous theorists—were attention through vision, communication through meaning, trust through positioning, and deployment of self through self-worth. The transformational components were "common universalities" of the surveyed executives and are combined in Tichy's 1984 transformational descriptors of creation of vision, mobilization of commitment, and institutionalization of change. Zalesnik in 1977 expressed charisma and consensus components as steps of visioning, the nature of work as an enabling force, the regard for others, and the sense of self [15].

Comparing the two types of leadership, the transactional style as an exchange process became more concerned with the follower in the aspect of consideration; one of the transactional aspects is contingent reinforcement, a more formalized type of interaction that implies an ongoing leader-follower relationship. Leadership by exception—a kind of patron system—hinges again on a sustained relationship with a follower and takes into account the initiating structure of the leader as opposed to some paternal or caretaking behaviors. Transformational leadership has, indeed, an initiating structure, one which is highly dependent upon consideration, evolving into a more aesthetic concern for people.

The judged quality of a transactional leader is strongly dependent upon the individual's group effectiveness in accomplishing expected transactions, given the inherent conflicts and complexities that develop in contingent situations, as follower need fluxes with the environmental impact and as leaders experience the need to orchestrate responses. Transformationally, much of the substance of the theory is that this type of leader's group effectiveness is a highly sequential, clearly outlined, and, ultimately, transcendental process of enabling followers to become empowered, envisioned, etc., by the provision for needs at much higher Maslovian levels than those served by transactional leadership.

There are political implications for transactional leaders in the interaction between situation and leader behavior; the reciprocity becomes once again more complex in the likely conflict of needs among followers in any given situation, or between follower(s) and situation and the event itself. This may limit the latitude of the leader to fulfill expectations; power may emerge as a one-way exchange process. Transformationally, however, leader behavior is less at the whim of any situation, since there is a constant sighting on the desired vision and perceived purpose that assesses the nature of an environmental event as it affects larger and more ethical aspects. There is a moral constancy, demonstrated in credibility, that serves as a touchstone for such leaders. Coming from the transformational repertoire of appropriate leader behaviors, a response to a situation is always compatible with the larger vision.

Continuing themes of transactional and transformational leadership that have common concepts are the vision capacity, the entrepreneurship, and the charisma as a compelling force and as a source of non-egotistical strength; all are distinct strands in the types of leadership required in Quality Management. Both in transactional and transformational leadership, the interaction between the leader and the follower is the fuel for organizational momentum, since leaders, in quality-driven organizations, have the primary roles of initiators, models, and coaches [16].

ENABLING BEHAVIORS AND BRIDGES TO NEW PRACTICE

Deming's original quality theory described the preeminent need for management to "create constancy of purpose for the improvement of product and service"; it is not a task to be delegated. The Total Quality philosophy is the primary responsibility of management; and leader initiation, maintenance, and participation are prerequisites. The absence of the traditional compliance and control-based management system is essential to a quality environment; leading becomes defined and practiced as helping, coaching, and supporting [9].

To facilitate this type of leader environment will require substantive retraining of traditional leaders/managers, as described in Chapter 2; training that should, possibly, precede an organization-wide adoption of Total Quality Management [17]. Key executive/administrator training, preferably in an off-site location, should be provided. Administrators can then begin to align their leadership style and thinking with TQM philosophy. Deliberate application practice may be needed if the concepts are substantively new or innovative to the existing leadership cadre. Professional consultation or facilitation services may be required in order to overcome fear of change and individual resistance [18].

SUMMARY

This chapter has considered theories of leadership as they evolved through the stages of: focus on traits and characteristics of leaders, the analysis of leaders' power and influence, behavioral approaches, the identification of situational factors that affect leaders, and more current transactional and transformational models. The theoretical formulations and research unfolding from these approaches to the study of leadership identify, compare, and determine the effectiveness of differing styles of leaders. In the trait focus, the attitudes and behaviors implied in the leadership trait findings point toward the leader qualities that enhance an entire organizational environment, with a holistic view of the organization and with the skillful management and maximization of human resources. Some of the most significant leader traits appear to be active participation, the creation of a facilitating climate, the provision of inspiration, the provision of justice and fairness, the resistance of unnecessary demands, the recognition of talent, and the exercise of ethical integrity. The leadership theory concerned with the source and amount of power and the way in which leaders use power, is described in two terms: position power and personal power. Position power is the formal authority inherent in the leader's office; by contrast, personal power is the potential influence stemming from the characteristics of the person in the office.

The behavioral approach focuses more on effective leader actions, rather than characteristics. The two dimensions of task/work orientation, known as initiating structure, and the interactive consideration, were described. Leader behavior as a focus was more developed and specific in its precision of description and in its initiation of consideration for the dynamics of behavior/style interacting with follower consideration and with its added third dimension of situation. Situational leadership involves concepts regarding the two dimensions of task/work orientation, known as initiating structure, and the interactive consideration for people. Contingency is a highly significant approach that is more complex to assess in the added dimensions; this involving the need for consideration and inclusion of multiple situational factors in the exercise of leadership.

A more striated and developmental type of model emerged in the transactional and transformational leadership designs. Transactional leadership is a type of situational and exchange process; transformational leadership has recurrent themes of charisma, empowerment, and visioning. Throughout the chapter, the relationship between leadership and quality was emphasized, stressing the primary role leaders must play in any Total Quality implementation.

REFERENCES

1. Bonstingl, J. J. 1992. *Schools of Quality: An Introduction to Total Quality Management in Education.* Alexandria, VA: Association for Supervision and Curriculum Development, pp. 42–43.
2. Hoy, W. K. and C. G. Miskel. 1987. *Educational Administration, Third Edition.* New York, NY: Random House, pp. 271–272.
3. Reiner, C. A. and H. Morris. 1987. "Leadership Development," in *Training and Development Handbook, Third Edition,* Robert L. Craig (ed.), New York, NY: McGraw-Hill, pp. 523–524.
4. Herman, J. J. 1991. "Coping with Conflict," *The American School Board Journal,* 178(8):26–28.
5. Herman, J. J. 1989. "Strategic Planning—One of the Changing Leadership Roles of the Principal," *The Clearing House,* 63(2):56–58.

6. Reiner and Morris, p. 525.

7. Herman, J. J. 1991. "Prerequisites for Instructional Leadership," in *Instructional Leadership Handbook, Second Edition*. Reston, VA: National Association of Secondary School Principals, pp. 99–103.

8. Hampton, D. R., C. E. Summer and R. A. Webber. 1987. *Organizational Behavior and the Practice of Management*. Glenview, IL: Scott, Foresman and Company, pp. 559–565.

9. Herman, J. J. 1991. "Confronting 'HOT' Issues Will Test President's Leadership Skills," *Michigan Association of School Boards Journal* (July/August):14, 15, 26, 29.

10. Hampton, Summer and Webber, pp. 564–575.

11. Hoy and Miskel, p. 76.

12. Herman, J. J. 1992. "Don't Do It Yourself: Delegation," *Executive Educator*, 14(11):26–27.

13. Herman, J. J. 1989. "Site-Based Management: Creating a Vision and Mission Statement," *NASSP Bulletin*, 73(519):79–83.

14. Herman, J. J. 1989. "A Vision for the Future: Site-Based Strategic Planning," *NASSP Bulletin*, 73(518):23–27.'

15. Hampton, Summer and Webber, pp. 577–578, 586–592, 595–596.

16. Kinlaw, D. C. 1992. *Continuous Improvement and Measurement for Total Quality*. San Diego, CA: Pfeiffer & Company, p. 82.

17. Herman, J. J. and G. McGiveron. 1987. "Administrative Magic: Turn Bureaucrats into Managers," *The American School Board Journal*, 174(2):32.

18. Jablonski, J. R. 1992. *Implementing TQM: Competing in the Nineties through Total Quality Management, Second Edition*. San Diego, CA: Pfeiffer & Company, pp. 67–72.

CHAPTER 4

Needs Assessment: A Prerequisite for Achieving Educational Quality Management

THIS chapter discusses (1) definition of the word *need*; (2) the use of mega, macro, and micro needs assessments; (3) district-level and building-level needs; (4) large and small group needs; (5) identifying the needs of individuals; (6) using a variety of needs assessments; (7) transformation of the identified needs into action programs; (8) enabling behaviors and bridges to new practice; and (9) theory-to-practice example.

A needs assessment is a starting point for further activities in any strategic and tactical planning process. The identification of needs – the gaps, based upon data between what is and what should or could be – is also an integral activity in the currently popular school improvement structures called: (1) Effective Schools, (2) Outcome-Based Education, (3) Total Quality Management, and (4) School-Based Management [1].

DEFINITION OF THE WORD *NEED*

A *need* is a gap or discrepancy between the current state of results and the desired future state of results. In other words, a need is a gap between *what is* and *what should or could be* [2]. It is not a wish, nor is it a desire; it is, instead, based upon a discrepancy analysis of factual information that discriminates between what is and what should or could be in terms of results.

Collectively, all identified gaps between what is and what should or could be the needs to be achieved become the preferred future vision for the school district and for the individual school buildings. A *preferred future vision* is the future state of results that are desired, and these desires are data-based results, which are determined by a comprehensive needs assessment [3,4]. Achieving the preferred future vision is not a short-term or quick-fix solution; it is a long-term commitment to eliminate all the gaps between what is and what should or could be.

In order to clarify the differences between needs and wishes and wants, let's look at three examples.

(1) We *wish* the school district's students would test higher on standardized tests. There is no data collected, nor is there a definition of how much higher students should score. Also, there is no indication of how to identify those students who must test higher and which norm-referenced or criterion-referenced tests are to be used.

(2) I *want* our high school's debate team to win the national debate competition in California. It would be wonderful for the students, school, school district, and community if this result became factual; but there is absolutely no factual data to back up this want.

(3) A *need* has been identified. Based on factual data, there has been a continuing increase of 1% per year over the last five years in the dropout rate of students in the district's four high schools. Today, the latest dropout rate stands at 16% of all high school students in the school district. Now that a need has been identified as a gap between what is and what should or could be, action plans can be initiated to attempt to obtain the desired future results. These action plans, once initiated, have to be closely monitored to determine if the results and effect desired, due to the action plan's interventions, are actually being achieved [5,6].

USING MEGA, MACRO, AND MIRCO NEEDS ASSESSMENTS

In order to fully identify the needs that should be addressed by a school district, it is important that the planners identify factors and trend data that relate to three differentiated types of needs. These three types include: (1) mega needs (societal), (2) macro needs (total organizational/school district), and (3) micro needs (individual school buildings, school departments, or other subunit) [7].

(1) *Mega needs* begin when the district's planners identify discrepancies (gaps) in the usefulness of what the organization delivers to society. Any rational person will never question that all societal organizations, including school districts, have a responsibility to assist in achieving certain societal needs.
  • *Example:* Attitudinal surveys conducted by the school district indicate that 85% of the district's high school students do not

feel that they have any obligation to others in their community or society.

- *One action plan:* Based upon the attitudinal survey data (soft data), the superintendent agreed with the faculty recommendation that the board adopt a policy to change the graduation requirements for students to include a compulsory Carnegie Unit of credit provided for a minimum of forty-five clock hours of community service. The students can do many community services: (1) assist in tutoring students having difficulty in school, (2) drive aged or handicapped residents to appointments and shopping trips, (3) help to paint houses for those who cannot afford the paint or lack the money to hire the help, (4) act as big brothers and big sisters to children from disengaged homes, (5) deliver meals to indigent residents, or (6) complete any other type of community service with prior approval of the coordinator of the community service program. The board of education agreed and adopted a board policy that included the above elements.
- *Monitoring and evaluating:* Periodically, at least yearly, a new attitudinal survey is administered to the high school students who have completed a minimum of forty-five hours of community service to determine whether they have a more positive attitude toward their individual obligations to provide service to their community.

(2) *Macro needs* begin with the identification of the gaps between what is and what should or could be in the results achieved by the total school district's organization.

- *Example:* The school district conducted a stratified random sampling telephone attitude poll of the residents of the community, and one of the most dramatic findings was that more than 96% of the respondents felt that they had no voice in the decisions made by the school district and that this left them with a negative attitude towards the school district and its decision makers. A follow-up survey of all teachers in the school district also had a similarly interesting finding.
- *One action plan:* The teachers indicated that they would prefer to have more decision-making authority for matters at the local school building level and that they would like parents and residents of the school's attendance area also to have more decision-making authority for matters related to the

local school building level. Because of the results of the attitudinal data, the administration recommended and the board of education adopted a policy creating a School-Based Management program that involved teachers, parents, nonparent residents, and the building principal in meaningful and numerous final decision making for the areas of instruction, personnel, building-level governance, and budget.

- *Monitoring and evaluating:* The results of repeat attitudinal surveys at the end of each year will provide evidence of whether the community residents and the teachers feel that they have a much more important voice in the decisions related to the district's schools and whether they are more inclined to look favorably upon the school district and its component schools.

(3) *Micro needs* begin with the gaps between what is and what should or could be in the results achieved by any subunit of the total organization (school district).

- *Example:* A review of standardized test scores over a period of the last five years reveals an increasing trend toward lesser student achievement scores in reading at the elementary level. Further investigation indicates that the districtwide summary masks the fact that one elementary school is causing the negative trend and that it has been increasingly impacted by *at-risk* students. In fact, this single elementary school, Edgemore Elementary, has more than 5% of the student body that is classified as at risk. Edgemore Elementary has 85% of its student body that could be classified as at-risk students.

- *One action plan:* The total action plan to overcome this identified need centers actions on the at-risk students of Edgemore Elementary. The Edgemore Elementary School is provided with two elementary counselors to assist the students with emotional adjustment problems. A tutorial program that enlists a citizen to work directly with an individual student under the direction of a teacher is also initiated. Finally, a full-time whole language specialist is assigned to Edgemore Elementary to work directly with the teachers to improve the reading delivery methods.

- *Monitoring and evaluating:* Annual standardized test results that are disaggregated for each school building and for every at-risk student will indicate whether there is a significant positive impact on students' achievement of the tri-method action program as evidenced by increasing reading test scores.

DISTRICT-LEVEL NEEDS AND BUILDING-LEVEL NEEDS

It is clear that, in order to improve the efficiency and effectiveness of any organization, including a school district, the parts and the whole have to be seen as a single interconnected system. In order for the system to be healthy, the needs have to be identified at both the building and total district levels; and action programs have to be implemented to make certain that the identified needs are met. That is, the gap results between what is and what should or could be are closed [8,9].

LARGE AND SMALL GROUP NEEDS

Not only should the needs of both the building level and central level be identified and programs developed to meet the identified needs; but, also, the needs that exist within large groups of students and employees and small groups of employees have to be identified [10,11]. Again, once they are identified, programs have to be developed to close the identified discrepancies between *what is* results and *what should or could be* results.

INDIVIDUALS' NEEDS

In addition to the obligation of planners to identify needs at the district and building levels, and at the large and small group levels, it is equally important to identify the needs that exist at the individual level [12,13]. Students are all individuals and many have unusual needs. Educators are required to devise an Individual Educational Plan (IEP) for each special education student, and an IEP for each student is devised to correct the identified individualized needs (gaps between the *what is* results and the *what should or could be* results). Using this concept and applying it to all students and all employees of the school district provide important keys to develop productive students and employees and to arrive at a productive, efficient, and effective school district [14,15].

A VARIETY OF NEEDS ASSESSMENT METHODS

There is no single best method of conducting a needs assessment. In fact, a combination of methods will best serve those individuals who are responsible for developing strategic, tactical, and operating plans to successfully meet the identified needs [16]. Both hard (factual) and soft (attitudinal or perceptual) data are helpful indicators of needs. Trends in these data over a lengthy time frame certainly provide clues to needs that should be addressed [17,18].

Some hard data and soft data examples that can prove useful in identifying district and building needs, large group and small group needs, and individuals' needs are identified below:

(1) Hard data: graduation rates, dropout rates, truancy rates, accidents, complaints, grievances, school grades, graduation, co-curricular activities, norm-referenced test results, and criterion-referenced test results
(2) Soft data: opinionnaires, attitude surveys, focus group discussions, telephone surveys, observational methods, and voting trends

TRANSFORMATION OF IDENTIFIED NEEDS INTO ACTION PROGRAMS

In order to develop a more effective and efficient school district's or school building's results, decision makers have to complete three functions: (1) conduct a needs assessment; (2) develop action programs designed to overcome the identified needs (gaps between what is and what should or could be); and (3) collect hard and/or soft data, monitor the results, and evaluate the level of success attained. All three of these functions have been discussed and illustrated above, but it is important at this juncture to stress that *all three functions* have to be completed for a district or school to become what its stakeholders desire it to become [19,20].

ENABLING BEHAVIORS AND BRIDGES TO NEW PRACTICE

The skills implied by implementation of the strategic and tactical planning process prerequisites described in this chapter are more staff development and human resource management in nature than may normally be expected to be possessed by the average school administrator, and this indicates a training agenda is needed. Many of the suggested activities in the described needs assessments would require initiation and support at the central office level (as is described in the following theory-to-practice example) and, in that sense, may frame more of a district-level blueprint prerequisite.

The training needed to create the mindset of mega, macro, and micro needs assessments and the skills required for the accumulation of data and the discernment of trends will require substantive resources. Effective and meaningful manipulation of the types of hard and soft data described previously will be needed to inform the development of action programs. It might be desirable, therefore, to initiate the needs assessment process on a pilot basis, and phase in districtwide training and facilitation.

THEORY-TO-PRACTICE EXAMPLE

Exceptional School District's decision makers have decided that a comprehensive needs assessment structure and process should be initiated for the school district. They also decided that a similar needs assessment should be conducted periodically for the purpose of identifying the preferred future vision for the school district when the current results data are compared to the desired results expectancy. The decision makers realized that a comprehensive needs assessment is a major element in creating a data base for strategic planning.

The Exceptional School District's decision makers decided on a multiple-step structure to arrive at a comprehensive needs assessment. The steps decided upon include:

- *Step one:* Decide on the partners to be included as part of the needs assessment operating team.
- *Step two:* The needs assessment team chooses to conduct a tri-level needs assessment that includes (1) mega (societal) needs, (2) macro (total organizational) needs, and (3) micro (subunit or individual) needs.
- *Step three:* Collect the hard and soft data bases from both external (outside the school district) and organizational (inside the school district) sources.

‣ *Step four:* List the identified needs that have been documented by data and agreed upon by the stakeholders involved in the planning group.

• *Step five:* Place all the needs in a priority listing and reconcile any disagreements between the data base and the statement of needs.

• *Step six:* List the priority needs to be attacked, and reach consensus with the planning partners on them.

• *Step seven:* Pass the identified, agreed upon, and prioritized needs on to the strategic, tactical, and operational planners who are responsible for developing programs to overcome the identified needs (gaps between what is and what should or could be).

Conducting a comprehensive needs assessment is not a quick task. It, like strategic planning, is a part of a long-term investment designed to improve the effectiveness and efficiency of the results achieved by the school district and its component schools.

SUMMARY

The prerequisites for achieving educational quality management were described in terms of determination of needs and the subsequent transformation into action programs. A need was defined as a gap between what is and what should or could be. Collective needs become the preferred future visions—the future desired state of results—which are data-based and become the basis for corresponding action plans. Examples were provided to clarify the difference between needs, wishes, and wants.

Three differentiated types of needs were identified: mega (societal), macro (total organizational/school district), and micro (individual school building, department, or other subunit). Examples of each of these needs and their corresponding action plans and monitoring and evaluation procedures were provided.

District-level and building-level needs were described as parts of a single, interconnected system, requiring action plans to meet these needs. Likewise, large and small group needs should be identified and served through action plans. Individual needs, those of students and employees, should be met; the concept of an IEP was presented as a model. A combination of needs assessment methods was recommended to best meet the array of currently identified needs and to determine longitudinal needs. Examples of hard and soft data were provided. The chapter concluded with a caveat concerning the three functions of needs determination and an example to illustrate it.

PRACTICAL EXERCISES

(1) Identify five needs for your school district for each of the three dimensions of needs assessment (total school district, subgroup, and individual).

(2) Project several felt needs for your school district, and briefly describe appropriate action plans for staff development activities to address those needs.

(3) Provide three examples of maintenance-related staff development activities, three examples of problem-solving staff development activities, and three examples of innovative staff development activities for your district.

(4) Collect district or school hard data within a defined area, such as math achievement in a particular group of students, and identify needs revealed by the data analysis.

(5) Collect any existing district or school soft data and determine if any needs or trends are revealed by it.

(6) Brainstorm with colleagues to determine which possible areas of need within the district are the most critical and deserving of resources dedicated to identify needs.

REFERENCES

1. Kaufman, R. 1988. *Planning Educational Systems: A Results-Based Approach.* Lancaster, PA: Technomic Publishing Company, Inc.

2. Herman, J. J. and J. L. Herman. In press. *Making Change Happen.* Newbury Park, CA: Corwin Press, Inc., a Sage Publications Company.

3. Kaufman, R. and J. J. Herman. 1991. "Strategic Planning for a Better Society," *Educational Leadership,* 48(7):4–8.

4. Lenz, R. and M. Lyles. 1986. "Managing Human Problems in Strategic Planning Systems," *Journal of Business Strategy,* 6:57–66.

5. Cawelti, G. 1987. "Strategic Planning for Curricular Reform," *Phi Kappa Phi Journal,* 67:29–31.

6. Knight, T. 1985. "Use Strategic Planning to Catapult Ideas into Action," *Executive Educator,* 7:21–22.

7. Herman, J. J. and R. Kaufman. 1991. "Making the Mega Plan," *The American School Board Journal,* 178(5):24–25, 41.

8. Cross, R. 1987. "Strategic Planning: What It Can and Can't Do," *Advanced Management Journal,* 52:13–16.

9. Morrisey, G., P. Below and B. Acomb. 1988. *The Executive Guide to Operational Planning.* San Francisco, CA: Jossey-Bass, Inc.

10. Herman, J. J. 1992. "Strategic Planning: Reasons for Failed Attempts," *Educational Planning,* 8(3):36–40.

11. Pfeiffer, J. (ed.). 1986. *Strategic Planning: Selected Readings.* San Diego, CA: University Associates, Inc.

12. Gilad, B. and T. Gilad. 1985. "Strategic Planning: Improving the Input," *Management Planning,* 33:10–13.

13. McCune, S. 1986. *A Guide to Strategic Planning for Educators.* Alexandria, VA: Association for Supervision and Curriculum Development.

14. Kaufman, R., J. J. Herman and K. Watters. Forthcoming. *Planning Educational Systems: What, When, How.* Lancaster, PA: Technomic Publishing Co., Inc.

15. Herman, J. J. 1989. "Strategic Planning—One of the Changing Leadership Roles of the Principal," *The Clearing House,* 63(2):56–58.

16. Herman, J. J. 1989. "A Vision for the Future: Site-Based Strategic Planning," *NASSP Bulletin,* 3(518):23–27.

17. Kaufman, R. and J. J. Herman. 1989. "Planning That Fits Every District: Three Choices Help Define Your Plan's Scope," *The School Administrator,* 46(8):17–19.

18. Dutton, J. and R. Duncan. 1987. "The Influence of the Strategic Planning Process on Strategic Change," *Strategic Management Journal,* 8:103–119.

19. Herman, J. J. 1989. "External and Internal Scanning: Identifying Variables That Affect Your School," *NASSP Bulletin,* 73(520):48–52.

20. Herman, J. J. 1990. "Action Plans to Make Your Vision a Reality," *NASSP Bulletin,* 74(523):14–17.

CHAPTER 5

Effective Schools Research: Building Blocks for High-Quality Strategic Goals for Schools

THIS chapter discusses (1) the Effective Schools Correlates, (2) potential uses of the Effective Schools Correlates, (3) designing action programs based upon the Effective Schools Correlates, (4) collecting impact and effectiveness data, (5) evaluating the action programs, (6) enabling behaviors and bridges to new practice, and (7) a theory-to-practice example.

THE EFFECTIVE SCHOOLS CORRELATES

During the last three decades, much interest has been centered on the requirement that our schools become more effective. Parallel with this interest, there has been a great deal of research geared to investigation of what can be done to make our schools more effective.

The research that has gained popular recognition is that derived from statistically significant findings related to the correlative research commonly referred to as Effective Schools Correlates. Stated simply, a positive *correlative* research result, in the case of effective schools, identifies the characteristics that exist in schools that are effective; and if these characteristics are absent or are not present to a sufficient degree, the schools are judged not to be effective. Correlative research findings are not considered by researchers as being as convincing evidence as *cause and effect* research, where statistical proof exists that when an identifiable variable is introduced into an environment, the desired effect (result) will occur to a statistically significant degree.

Correlative research findings are valuable to the field of education, as well as to many of the social sciences, and are very helpful in determining directions that a school district and its component schools can take to improve the education of the children for whom they carry responsibility. The Effective Schools researchers have found specific correlates that are associated with schools that are judged to be effective. These statistically significant findings are listed below:

- *Strong instructional leadership is present in those schools that are effective.* Effective principals are crucial to the development of effective schools. They are actively involved in monitoring student achievement, curriculum planning, staff development, and all issues related to instruction and the welfare of students. They also have and sell a clear vision of what their school should be, and they involve important stakeholders in the development of a mission, goals, and specific measurable objectives.
- *A safe and orderly school climate is present, and it is conducive to a learning environment.* Many climate studies indicate that effective schools possess both a safe and orderly climate, one that exudes a caring and high expectation attitude toward students.
- *High expectations for students' achievements are held by teachers and administrators.* These high expectations for students' achievements are evidenced by (1) the format of classroom management, (2) the time spent on instructional tasks, and (3) the expectation of mastery learning by each student. There exists an intense focus on instructional results.
- *High emphasis is placed on the mastery of basic skills by all students in the areas of reading, writing, mathematics, and language arts.* If mastery is achieved on these basics, many believe that it will also influence student achievement in other curricular areas. Mastery achievement on each of these is, indeed, an instructional outcome to be valued, and maximizing the instructional time spent by students on these academic-related tasks is also important to the achievement of student mastery.
- *Monitoring of each student's progress continues, and regular feedback is provided in those schools considered to be effective.* Data on the academic achievement of each student and of the total student body is systematically collected, monitored, arrayed in understandable and usable format, and provided as feedback to all parties. These data are utilized by all teachers and by all students, and they are distributed to parents and guardians as an effective means of two-way communication.

Both standardized norm-referenced test results and criterion-referenced test results are utilized. Norm-referenced tests are item analyzed for item specific results related to the achievement of each student and the entire student body. Criterion-referenced test results are reviewed to determine if each student has achieved mastery on the specific results that were predetermined to be desired.

The data from both types of student tests are disaggregated to determine the achievement patterns that may differ among the sexes, socioeconomic levels, students at risk, and all other subcategories that will assure that *each* student's achievement level will not be masked by some generalized average score. Each student is considered a valued and important product, and teachers and administrators truly believe that each student must achieve well in school if she/he is to become a productive citizen and a confident individual.

• *Parent and community involvement exist in those schools that are determined to be effective.* If parents and community members and community organizations are supportive of vision, mission, goals, objectives, and procedures of the schools, this support enhances the probability of the schools becoming and remaining effective. If the same individuals and groups are not supportive of their schools, the chances of successful student achievement and employee effectiveness will probably be diminished [1,2].

POTENTIAL USES OF THE EFFECTIVE SCHOOLS CORRELATES

As an organizational framework and as a viable school improvement model, the Effective Schools Correlates' language and knowledge base can be used as a basis for collegial dialogue and as an organizing framework for school improvement [3]. More significantly, as will be seen in later chapters, they can meaningfully support the strategic planning process and, by the very nature of their customer-driven content, likewise fit into and give meaning to a Total Quality Management process.

DESIGNING ACTION PROGRAMS BASED UPON THE EFFECTIVE SCHOOLS CORRELATES

Action plans are those operational plans that clearly and comprehensively set out tasks and procedures to accomplish a particular objective [4]. Most of the school improvement projects that have been undertaken in the last decade have included elements of Effective Schools research and common practice [5]. Action plans that are designed around this theoretical framework demand specific strategies and activities to support each of the described correlates, which will later be interwoven with the goals and objectives of the strategic plan's blueprint (see Chapter 9). Effective Schools–driven action plans that support the district's strategic plan, in the areas of school climate, management, instruction, and curricular goals and objectives, will then become part of the holistic Quality Management process.

For each of the correlates, assessments can be made as to the perceptions and needs of the stakeholders. For example, the school's instructional leadership "temperature" can be taken through the use of appropriate instrumentation and interviews—the gathering of hard and soft data—in order to determine what strengths the organization possesses and what needs must be met with regard to the management of instruction [6]. As part of the overall action plan, specific strategies and activities can then be developed to meet those needs.

In order to initiate an action plan for Effective Schools–based implementation, a marketing approach aimed at creating awareness of the action planning process should be developed. Representative stakeholders (staff, parents, and community members) should be involved in the planning. The introduction and initiation of such plans should motivate and involve school personnel by establishing the commitment of leadership and by assigning roles and responsibilities as the development of implementation game plans for the school begins. Timelines and the setting for this will be determined by the school calendar and by the timelines set by the district strategic plan. A retreat setting can enhance a desirable sense of collegiality and provide a quality-focused effect.

COLLECTING IMPACT AND EFFECTIVENESS DATA

A targeted and individual school-specific assessment and systematic collection of hard and soft data, including instructionally current practices and attitudes, must be done in order to identify the strengths, needs, and resources. In order to work as an Effective Schools/school improvement planning team, teachers and other professionals will need the data base created by the achievement and other information available. This type of hard data should include [1]:

- campus size, enrollment, and profiles of staff members
- gender, ethnic, and students' family structure types
- stability and turnover indicators: creating cohorts of students arranged by length of time enrolled at the school
- student conduct: numbers and percent relating to categories of disciplinary action, from initial actions to suspensions and expulsions
- attendance by grading periods
- standardized test data and grades per class or subject per grading period
- levels of participation in student activities and types of participation, such as student government and athletics
- parental involvement statistics: PTA membership, volunteer numbers and hours, nature of parental participation in school activities
- professional growth of staff: topics, hours, and numbers participating
- staff attendance
- informal data, such as opinionnaires, parent perceptions, etc.

The key point about this data, if it is to be meaningful with regard to school improvement and Effective Schools research, is that it *be disaggregated by gender, by ethnic group, and by the socioeconomic status of students.* Unless the trends of subpopulations are revealed, the school's action planning team cannot identify specific areas of nonperformance or group need [8]. For example, if there is language underachievement among sixth grade girls or if there is overrepresentation of a certain socioeconomic group (usually as determined by Chapter I or Free and Reduced Lunch family income eligibility information) in elected student government ranks or if one particular age-cohort of students shows a longitudinal tendency for problems in math skills, such information is important to action planners as they consider ways to implement the Effective Schools Correlates. Similarly, the data should be disaggregated for programmatic analysis, using such categories as the achievement and attitudinal information about the groups of students participating in such differentiated programs as Chapter I, special education, gifted and talented, or English as a Second Language (ESL). Programmatic data should likewise be disaggregated by gender, ethnic group, and socioeconomic status of students.

As described previously, there is instrumentation available, which probes the perceptual levels of students, teachers, other employees, and parents about the existence and the levels of quality of each of the Effective Schools Correlates; school climate assessment instruments, indeed, are abundantly available. This type of information should be gathered and disaggregated, as described above. Likewise, teacher, other employee, and parent information should be particularly analyzed for any grade level or class/subject area trends [9].

This array of data, already analyzed for trends and discernible directions/patterns by a committee(s) charged with this purpose, should be shared with the entire staff prior to coming together as an action planning team. The strategic goals and objectives of the district (to be addressed in Chapter 9), and any action plans that have been designed to meet them, should be shared as well. With constant reference to the district strategic perspective and informed by the array of school trends and current/longitudinal data, the school's action planners can collectively begin to set their own goals and objectives with regard to implementing the Effective Schools practices. These should be determined on a schoolwide basis and, in a corresponding and supportive manner, by each grade level, department, or program area.

It is advisable that a collective quality and articulation check be done, realigning the selected goals and objectives with the district strategic plan and classifying each goal and objective under one or more of the Effective Schools Correlates, and that officially, the final action plans are approved and adopted as a school. Each grade level and department should then meet individually to determine the collective classroom activities that will support the action plans of the adopted Effective Schools goals and objectives.

EVALUATING THE ACTION PROGRAMS

Within the school setting, it may be helpful to create monitoring structures or committees framed around the Effective Schools Correlates. These should be cross-grade level or interdepartmental to maintain a whole-school and collegial view of the implementation of the action plan process. Each committee can set up ways to monitor the implementation of its correlate-related strategies, such as information-gathering visits with school individuals or groups, monitoring of grade averages per subject per subpopulation at predetermined intervals, or frequent correlate-related informal assessment instruments to check on perceived levels and sense of quality of the Effective Schools improvement implementation. These committees can report on a scheduled basis to the whole school, at staff or other meetings, or through written communiqués.

At the principal and central office level, there should be overall facilitation (through consultation with groups, logistical arrangements, purchasing, arranging for training, etc.) and monitoring of the action plan. The proposed support of the grade level/departmental and individual activities and objectives should be incorporated into the staff evaluation process and should be included in the overall action plan and in a timeline format. It would be helpful if each of the grade levels/departments had a similar action plan, developed with the assistance of the principal. As the results of standardized tests are returned at various times during the year, an organized distribution plan should facilitate the dissemination of the scores to each grade level/department and to parents/stakeholders. Since they usually reflect total school data, the entire staff should meet to trend analyze, compare, and link them with previous longitudinal test data to determine if any revision of the predetermined Effective Schools improvement strategies is warranted.

An ongoing data gathering process should be in place. As the Effective Schools committees gather anecdotal and informal soft data information, as student grades accumulate over the various grading periods, and as standardized test data come in, they should be stored for the end of the school year staff review. Predetermined evaluative action plan techniques (such as follow-up informal assessment about the presence and quality of each of the Effective Schools Correlates, measures of percentile gains in specific areas of norm-referenced tests, and end-of-year grade level and subject area averages of disaggregated groups) should be applied, and the resulting array of outcomes and accomplishments again realigned and compared with the selected goals and objectives of the district strategic plan [10].

ENABLING BEHAVIORS AND BRIDGES TO NEW PRACTICE

The processes described here for initiating and fully implementing an Effective Schools, quality-driven improvement model [11], one which would be shaped by the strategic and tactical planning described in Chapter 9, would possibly require a substantive attitudinal change on the part of the stakeholders and the participants in the individual schools. Certainly, staff development, aimed at creating awareness of and commitment to the Effective Schools concepts, would be needed. However, a more specific training regimen may be represented by the skills demanded in the process itself: the time and expertise to gather data; the collaborative and whole-school–focused planning and assessment procedures; and the need for creative and flexible responses to the emerging needs of the organization. Certainly, the Total Quality elements of continuous improvement and total organizational focus are implied in the described process.

It is advisable, in view of the mass of possible innovative practices and unfamiliar attitudes required by this process, to facilitate the behaviors and provide the transitions to new practice in an incremental fashion. The skills described here are those which will also be recommended and required in later chapters.

THEORY-TO-PRACTICE EXAMPLE

Before detailing an abbreviated practical example of a school using the Effective Schools research, let's identify a model that will indicate the interconnections and supplemental details to assist in the implementation of the basic correlates of effective schools.

AN EFFECTIVE SCHOOLS MODEL

Desired Outcomes	Instruction	Management
1. Productive citizens	1. High expectations for students' achievement	1. Clear, preferred vision and mission
2. Student mastery	2. Mastery learning	2. Strategic goals
	3. Quality curricula	3. Tactical action plans
	4. Research-based delivery methods	4. Time on task
	5. Monitoring of students' progress and feedback	5. Safe and orderly school climate

Desired Outcomes	Instruction	Management
	6. Classroom climate	6. Strong instructional leadership
	7. Time on task	7. Parent and community involvement
		8. Focus on students' achievement

With the details of the model in mind, it is important to illustrate the use of Effective Schools research by providing an abbreviated example. The hypothetical Successful Middle School will be used to illustrate how decision makers at the school can develop its plans to improve its school and its students' achievement.

Successful Middle School

The Successful Middle School's preferred future *vision* includes the following:

- Parents and residents of the school's attendance areas shall be included in the decision-making process of the school, and they shall be supporters of the students and the educational programs.
- High-achieving students and employees are the expected norm at this school.
- The environment of the school will be not only safe and orderly, but it will also be caring and will emphasize success by students, employees, and the school's community residents.
- Strong instructional leadership shall be provided by all teachers and by all administrators connected with the school.
- Continual monitoring of student achievement levels will be conducted, and the results will be used to make desired improvements in the instructional delivery systems.

Once the preferred future vision has been determined, a *mission statement* should be agreed upon by the stakeholders' planning group.

The mission of Successful Middle School is that of providing quality instruction that will allow our students to achieve at a high level, which, in turn, will enable them to be very successful when they enter senior high school; and parents and community members will be involved in assisting in achieving this mission.

When the vision and mission have been determined the next planning step is that of stating strategic goals. Three of the most important goals developed for Successful Middle School include:

- Students will regularly attend school, and they will arrive at school in a timely manner.
- Each student will achieve at a high level of academic achievement.
- Each student will achieve at a minimum of one year's level of achievement or at a greater than one year's level of achievement in all basic subjects for each year of attendance at Successful Middle School.

Once the strategic goals are determined, they should spell out the desired results of *what should be*. Once the what should be results have been determined, they can be compared to the current level, or the *what is* level, of achievement in the goal areas. The discrepancy or gap between the what should be and the what is levels of results determines the *needs* to be addressed. In other words, a need is the gap or discrepancy that exists between the what should be and the what is state of affairs in the school related to the strategic goals.

Once the strategic goals are developed, specific measurable objectives must be developed. Using the above strategic goals and the needs assessment data, the stakeholders' planning committee developed the following specific objectives:

- *Specific objective one:* By the end of the year, the student absentee and tardiness rates will be lessened by a minimum of 25% when compared to identical data from the previous school year.
- *Specific objective two:* As a group, student improvement will increase by a minimum of 5% over the past three years' pattern; and, within five years, there will be a decrease of a minimum of 30% in the number of individual students who are achieving below their grade level.

Once the specific objectives are determined, action programs must be developed. Action programs initiated by the stakeholders' planning committee at Successful Middle School related to specific objective one include: (1) opening the schools before and after school for a latchkey program for working parents, (2) establishing a call to the home system every day for every student who is absent or tardy, and (3) providing a monthly assembly for the purpose of providing certificates to students who have had improved attendance records and for providing an even higher level of recognition for students who have had perfect attendance for the month and for the school year to date.

The stakeholders' committee developed the following action plans related to specific objective two: (1) an after-school study program was initiated, which included a school-based study room manned by voluntary teachers; (2) a telephone student assistance system manned by teachers, administrators, and trained volunteers; and (3) a daily homework and testing procedure for each class.

The action programs detailed the answers to the following questions:

- Why is this tactic being implemented?
- Who is responsible for the achievement of each task to bring this program into operation?
- What specifically is to become part of this program?
- How will this program be implemented?
- When will this program be implemented?
- Where will this program be housed?
- What resources will be provided to implement this program?
- How will one determine if the results of this program meet the expectations?

Once the action plans are decided upon, the next task becomes one of collecting formative and summative data of both the hard and soft variety. These data, then, can be used to decide whether or not the program attempted is at a satisfactory level, whether the program should be continued or eliminated, or whether there are some modifications to be made that will improve the program as it is implemented in the future.

SUMMARY

This chapter has presented an implementation model of the Effective Schools concepts, with an emphasis on the corresponding action plans. The key Effective Schools concepts include the following: (1) strong instructional leadership is provided; (2) a safe and orderly concept that is conducive to learning exists; (3) expectations of high-level academic achievement by *each* student are held by teachers and administrators; (4) great emphasis is placed on the *mastery* of basic skills; (5) norm-referenced and criterion-referenced achievement test results are analyzed in detail for each student, feedback is provided to each student and teacher, and the results are utilized to improve instruction; and (6) parents, community members, and community groups are involved with and supportive of the schools in a positive manner.

A description of the potential uses of the correlates was followed by suggestions for action plans designed around that theoretical framework, with specific strategies and activities to support each of the described correlates. There was recommended inclusion of a myriad of hard and soft data in a Management Information System. The importance of disaggregating data into demographic and programmatic categories to achieve detail of display and to facilitate stakeholder trend analysis was emphasized. Structures for monitoring and evaluating the improvement process were framed around the Effective Schools Correlates, including formal and informal checkpoints, review of hard and soft data as it accumulated over the academic year, and the continuous review of such information, as is done in Total Quality Management. A description of recommended enabling behaviors and bridges to new practice preceded a theory-to-practice middle school example.

PRACTICAL EXERCISES

(1) Describe examples of evidence, if any, of each of the correlates in your school or district.
(2) Decide which correlate is least evident, and design a staff development outline of training, which might strengthen the presence of that correlate in your school or district.
(3) What evidences of built-in monitoring structures exist in your district?
(4) Are there any other existing structures in the district that might facilitate and enhance the presence of the correlates?

REFERENCES

1. Lezotte, L. W. (speaker). 1989. *Effective Schools Videotapes* (videotape recordings). Okemos, MI: Effective Schools Products.

2. Brookover, W. et al. 1982. *Creating Effective Schools: An Inservice Program for Enhancing School Learning Climate and Achievement.* Holmes Beach, FL: Learning Publications, Inc.
3. Lezotte, L. 1989. *Effective Schools Research Abstracts.* Okemos, MI: Effective Schools Products.
4. Kaufman, R. and J. Herman. 1991. *Strategic Planning in Education.* Lancaster, PA: Technomic Publishing Co., Inc., p. 246.
5. Herman, J. J. and J. L. Herman. 1993. *School Based Management: Current Thinking and Practice.* Springfield, IL: Charles C. Thomas, Publisher, pp. 228–230.
6. Newman, F. et al. 1991. *National Center on Effective Secondary Schools' Final Report on OERI Grant No. G-00869007.* Madison, WI: Wisconsin Center for Education Research.
7. Herman, J. J. and J. L. Herman. In press. *Making Change Happen.* Newbury Park, CA: Corwin Press.
8. Levine, D. 1991. "Creating Effective Schools: Findings and Implications for Research and Practice," *Phi Delta Kappan,* 72(5):389–393.
9. Duden, N. 1993. "A Move from Effective to Quality," *School Administrator,* 50(5):18–21.

CHAPTER 6

Outcome-Based Education: Potential Usage as an Educational Quality Management Measurement Delivery System for Schools

THIS chapter discusses (1) defining Outcome-Based Education (OBE); (2) elaborating the specific characteristics of the Outcome-Based Education movement; (3) determining the three levels of results: products, outputs, and outcomes; (4) utilizing outcomes as measurables; (5) enabling behaviors and bridges to new practice; (7) theory-to-practice example, and (8) current OBE status and conclusion.

Outcome-Based Education is an approach to schooling that has come about as a result of the emphasis on student success, which was born of the 1980's decade of reform and restructuring and results from the national emphasis on the academic lag of American students in international educational achievement levels. Spady and Marshall describe three forces that have impacted this restructuring. In the past decade, states and districts have instituted such learning project improvements as Mastery Learning and the Outcomes-Driven Developmental Model; regional and state policy-making bodies have included improved student outcomes in the 1991 National Goals for America's Schools, centering them in the concurrent efforts of changes in curriculum, instruction, assessment, attendance, credentialing, accreditation, and accountability; and a growing consensus of educators, private sector leaders, and political leaders support the call for a new, restructured educational system that is philosophically based in success and outcome based in practice [1].

Changes in society have meant that the traditional outcomes of the educational system—success for some and failure for many others—are significantly more problematic than they were in previous decades, due to the diminishing employment possibilities of the contemporary job environment. By contrast, OBE emphasizes organizing for results and is a deliberate attempt to "plan and conduct essential activities so as to accomplish our aims successfully—in other words, purposefully doing what we set out to do" [2]. Some definitions of OBE, which more clearly illustrate these notions, follow.

DEFINING OUTCOME-BASED EDUCATION

Many descriptions exist for Outcome-Based Education; most are framed around the notion of the need for structural change in schools—to move from a system that is clock-and-calendar defined to one that is mastery in model and focuses on aptitude as a concept that involves a student's learning *rate,* rather than a student's learning *level.* A variety of definitions exist from several sources within the professional literature and practice.

OBE has been defined as a "system of instructional and management practices that, when followed carefully and consistently, have been found to increase student achievement significantly." It can be further defined as "a comprehensive approach to managing instruction, people, and resources for the desired outcomes of education—increased learning and high achievement" [3]. It has also been described as "organizing for results, basing what we do instructionally on the outcomes we want to achieve, whether in specific parts of the curriculum or in the schooling process as a whole" [4]. Outcome-Based Instruction, a companion term that occurs in the literature, can be defined as focusing on successful learning outcomes for virtually all students [5].

General elements of a working OBE definition can be discerned: a change from the current temporally driven structure, an obvious connection to classic Mastery Learning in its emphasis on success for all students, and a wide range of implementation latitude, with clearly defined outcomes and expectations—the holding of schools as accountable only for product quality, not for procedural and process compliance. Deming's features of quality are evident in OBE if student learning is viewed as the core production process and the instructional system facilitating that learning is viewed as the work processes of the rest of the organization, designed to enable and enhance that core function [6]. The connections with Total Quality Management are evident in the commitment to quality outcome and customer satisfaction, in the quality specifications contained in the clearly defined services and products, in the strategic planning required to map the route to success for all students, and in the quality assurance component of assessment of outcomes [7].

ELABORATING THE SPECIFIC CHARACTERISTICS OF THE OUTCOME-BASED EDUCATION MOVEMENT

Practitioners of OBE use the starting point of determining the knowledge, competencies, and qualities that they want students to be able to demonstrate when they finish their education—to determine, in other words, the "exit outcomes," which are the result of "designing, developing, delivering, and documenting instruction in terms of its intended goals and outcomes" [8]. In order to reach outcomes successfully, it is necessary to accommodate differences in learning rates and to focus on a coaching style of delivery that results in a range of times needed to reach given outcomes, rather than the relative success levels of those outcomes at common points in time—a bottom-up curricular approach. OBE combines two curricular approaches: fidelity (adherence to a common core content) and adaptivity (the interpretation of that content translated into meaningful practice within classroom settings). While the exact instructional outcomes are explicitly stated, the means to those ends are the purview of the instructional planner [9]. The curriculum is therefore developed from the outcomes, which can be more global, high-level, and cross-disciplinary in nature, rather than simply being expressed in functional and basic skill terms. The curricular design direction is downward, a direct parallel to the visioning process in strategic planning.

Outcome-Based Education has been described as founded on three basic premises [10]:

- All students can learn and succeed, though not necessarily at the same time and in an identical fashion.
- Success breeds success.
- Schools can control the conditions for such success.

Also, three key operational principles are related to OBE's success conditions: a clarity of focus on outcomes, expanded opportunity and instructional support, and high expectations for learning success. Students are provided with clear descriptions for acceptable performance criteria, are supported by an intensive coaching atmosphere with careful assessment of prerequisite learnings and by a focus on outcomes validated by demonstration, and are held to high standards with no defined limits on opportunities for grade improvements [11]. Additionally, specific criteria for OBE have been adopted by the Network for Outcome Based Schools, a grant-funded organization founded in 1980. The Network, committed to implementing a culture of success for all, has approved the following school standards [12], which also serve as OBE characteristics:

(1) A collectively endorsed mission that reflects staff commitment to

essential exit outcomes and the implementation of conditions which maximize opportunities for success

(2) Clearly defined, publicly derived exit outcomes that reflect the contemporary knowledge and competencies required for successful adulthood and that are successfully demonstrated by all students

(3) A tightly articulated curriculum framework of program, course, and unit outcomes that are derived from exit outcomes, which integrate knowledge, competence, and orientations across domains of learning and that directly facilitate exit outcomes

(4) A system of instructional decision making and delivery that consistently assures successful demonstration of all student outcomes, makes needed instruction available on a timely basis throughout the calendar year, employs a rich diversity of instruction within a transformational Mastery Learning framework, and deliberately provides multiple avenues for student success

(5) A criterion-based, consistently applied system of assessments, performance standards, student credentialing, and reporting that is closely aligned with outcomes, generates intrinsic motivation for high levels of performance, documents student success and improvement at flexible times, and prevents individual comparisons

(6) A system of instructional organization and delivery that enables students to advance through curriculum at an individual rate and to meet eligibility criteria in a timely manner through a Mastery Learning framework

(7) A system that recognizes the power of organizational culture on staff and student development and that creates a climate that enables all students to perform at high-quality levels

(8) An ongoing system of program improvement that expands the staff vision of potential goals and operations, staff accountability for the results of professional decisions and practices, and staff capacities for effective leadership, performance, and renewal/change

(9) A data base of course and unit outcomes for all students and other indicators of school effectiveness, which is used to update and improve conditions and practices that affect student and staff success

The attributes of OBE correspond to Schlecty and Sizer's school restructuring elements, in that it is collaborative, flexible, cross-disciplinary, outcome-based, open in systemic structure, and distinguished by an empowerment component. Advanced OBE models are distinguished by their focus on a framework of exit outcomes that address the concept of the graduate as a total person, rather than the more traditional OBE models, which tend to focus on the transformation of existing subject area curricula into a mastery format, with no consideration given to the real-life desired outcomes [13].

DETERMINING THE THREE LEVELS OF RESULTS: PRODUCTS, OUTPUTS, AND OUTCOMES

In Outcome-Based Education, the focus on outcomes is tied to successful demonstration of learning, which occurs at some culminating point in a student's learning experiences. The demonstration may be of a more application-oriented and tangible nature, such as an academic product of some sort: an original computer program design, a position paper, or a problem/solution science design. These demonstrations may be viewed as products, while the more affective and behavioral learning outcome applications, such as the demonstrated capacity for self-directed learning and for functioning within culturally diverse settings, may be viewed as outputs. Both are building blocks of more broadly defined and goal-oriented *outcomes*.

A more concrete way to view these building blocks is a hierarchy of outcomes: program outcomes, course outcomes, unit outcomes, and lesson outcomes. All, however, should be derived from the overarching exit outcomes, which are the "most broad level of what students should know, be able to do, and to be like when they leave our schools" [14]. The increasing level of specificity would determine the type of assessment.

Four key principles of OBE frame the three levels of results [15]. The ensuring of clarity of focus on significant outcomes is supported by the cumulation of demonstrations of mastery, which may take the form of products (such as an acceptable writing portfolio) or outputs (such as the demonstration of interpersonal skills in collaborative decision making). These smaller building blocks underlie the larger program outcomes, which could be expressed in such role-defined terms as students functioning as perceptive thinkers, collaborative contributors, or innovative producers. The design of ultimate outcomes drives the subsequent design of culminating demonstrations of mastery. The emphasis on high expectations for all permeates all three types of results. The provision of expanded opportunity and support for learning success is intended to give temporal and instructional flexibility to the attainment of outcomes through the smaller stepping stones of products and outputs.

UTILIZING OUTCOMES AS MEASURABLES

Student attainment of OBE's designated outcomes is dependent upon a testing program that is congruent with the school curriculum. After an initial baseline assessment, the concept of *value-added* is incorporated into the education process, as each student is evaluated on terminal objectives that support agreed-upon outcomes. It is recommended that assessment procedures meet the criteria of reliability, validity, discrimination, and efficiency—ensuring that those procedures measure the skills intended and distinguish between mastery and non-mastery of the learning outcome. Applied performance objectives, as well as more traditional assessment methods, are used, as described earlier in the distinction made between products, outputs, and outcomes [16].

The validation of OBE-style student achievement is based upon the defined outcome attainment, rather than the time-based set of grading procedures. For example, course content that may have taken a student a semester to attain entry level and a summer to successfully complete is reflected on a transcript as the summer grade only [17].

Such measurables are used not only to determine mastery and outcome attainment, but also to form instructional groupings around readiness level and task needs, which are further defined in the following sections.

ENABLING BEHAVIORS AND BRIDGES TO NEW PRACTICE

Since the visioning of desired outcomes is a critical component of OBE, the strategic planning process, which emphasizes the development of vision and mission, is a logical connection and a prerequisite for implementation. Exit outcomes must be developed, and the ownership and commitment that facilitate that development must be in place. Training teachers to use the OBE instructional process, with emphasis on Mastery Learning and best instructional research, is a must. The implied recycling and grouping of instruction in the OBE model demands some accommodation of teaching behaviors. Likewise, its holistic and more interdisciplinary and collaborative teaching structure demands some innovative strategies for facilitation. The formation of building teams to monitor the integrity of implementation assists this process. Principals will need support and training to facilitate this implementation.

Overall, a district should lay the groundwork for OBE through a number of processes. Board adoption of the model and subsequent ownership and commitment are critical. The vision and beliefs system, and the accompanying outcomes structure, must be clear to all and embedded in each building. The cooperation and involvement of union membership and leadership and parental stakeholders is vital [18].

Implementation of OBE demands some massive curriculum development effort to "design down" from the exit outcomes, translating them into specific lesson outcomes. Attention must be paid to the logistics of enrichment and remediation, to special needs students, and to the mechanics of monitoring the progress of students. The process of moving a school district from traditional practice into OBE demands all of the usual change facilitations, particularly if the implementation is one component of a larger restructuring design for quality education [19]. Therefore, a process for change is needed to enable implementation, and a staff development model provided for facilitation of continual renewal. Problem-solving procedures and climate-monitoring policies should be in place. The instructional process for OBE must have the endorsement of the entire staff, and the organization of the curriculum should be consistent with that instructional process. Such practices as grouping and the how-to's of certification of student learning (demonstration of mastery) must be determined by consensus. Classroom practices in such areas as testing, grading, homework, incomplete assignments, and in organizational structure, such as mainstreaming, must be cooperatively developed and aligned [20].

THEORY-TO-PRACTICE PATTERNS

Many districts have implemented OBE, sometimes as a part of larger restructuring, sometimes as part of a state department invitational effort, and sometimes as an individual district project. Typically, the implementation has involved awareness and the development of the planning phase of the desired outcomes design through staff development, frequently initiating the change through a core group, whose members serve as trainers and facilitators to each school. A voluntary and phased-in process was occasionally used.

The objectives (outcomes) are developed for each grade level and content area and are matrixed from level to level to maintain continuity in skill building and to guard against overlap and omission. Curricular alignment — teaching the essentials that were to be tested for mastery and assessing that which was actually taught — is a recommended practice. Task analysis for the newly determined outcomes should be done to clarify the readiness levels and prerequisites for instructional objectives and outcomes. Formative assessments are prepared to identify students requiring correctives, and extensions are developed for those demonstrating mastery.

Computer software to manage the student mastery record keeping and the program coordination is frequently used, framed around the objectives and outcomes determined by the district and capable of generating lists of students eligible for instruction on particular objectives. The fluid formation of classes around task needs seems complex, but the involvement of the entire instructional staff in teaching math, for example, can be coordinated; this organizational flexibility works through block scheduling at the secondary level. Assignment of teachers to the constantly changing and reforming group allows for individual preference of teachers for a relatively stable assignment or a variety of instructional settings [21–23].

CURRENT OBE STATUS AND CONCLUSION

The concept of OBE, conceived in the Johnson City, New York, schools in the early 1970s, which ultimately resulted in the National Center for Outcome Based Education, has developed into a basic form, the Outcomes Driven Developmental Model (ODDM). Essential components of this more evolved and later model include the following [24]:

- ODDM addresses all of the major requirements and expectations of restructuring.
- ODDM specifies clear, observable, and measurable outcomes for every experience. These include exit learner behaviors, program outcomes, course outcomes, and lesson outcomes.

- In ODDM, change is accepted as a normal part of living within a dynamic organization. All aspects of a school's operations are constantly reviewed and are subject to change.
- Every member of the organization has the opportunity to influence decision making from best knowledge. Knowledge, rather than position, determines a person's ability to influence.
- Expectations of quality and excellence are maintained at a high level. All school members are trained and supported to achieve quality.
- There is a commitment and a strenuous training and support system in place to assist each person to move successfully from theory to the precise behaviors, skills, and attitudes that make total success possible.
- The ODDM process is a holistic, total systems approach. Everything is interconnected and interactive. Fragmentation of effort is never acceptable.
- ODDM creates an environment that satisfies needs. Each person is valued, nurtured, and given the opportunity to develop.

Several essential elements of Total Quality Management can be discerned in this list. Deming's quality feature of the efficacy of frequent, informed interaction between the worker and the object of the work and between the workers and the processes that support them are evident. Quality results require consistent leadership, effective systemic management, and a common belief-based framework for understanding among all members of the system; these requirements comprise the essence of Outcome-Based Education [25,26].

SUMMARY

The chapter described Outcome-Based Education as emphasizing success and results, a movement born of the decade of reform and restructuring. Its definitions were framed around the concept of a need for structural change in school. Outcome-Based Education was described as a system of instructional and management practices aimed at increasing learning and high achievement, which focuses on aptitude as a concept affecting learning rate, rather than level. As a concept, it was also described as having obvious connections to Mastery Learning and to some elements of Total Quality Management. The specific characteristic of the OBE movement is the variability of the rates at which learners achieve given outcomes, rather than the relative success levels of those outcomes at common points in time. It is founded on the basic premises of the ability of all students to learn, that success breeds success, and that schools can facilitate such success.

Also, three key operational principles related to OBE's success conditions were provided: a clarity of focus on outcomes, expanded opportunity and instructional support, and high expectations for learning success. Additionally, the specific criteria for OBE that were adopted by the Network for Outcome Based Schools were listed, including standards on mission, exit outcomes, an articulated curriculum and individualized instruction, a consistent system of assessment, a program improvement component, and a data base for update.

OBE's focus on outcomes was described as tied to successful demonstrations of learning, which may be viewed as products, while the more affective and behavioral learning outcome applications were viewed as outputs; both are building blocks and goal-oriented. The consequent validation of OBE-style student achievement was described as based upon the defined outcome attainment, rather than the time-based set of grading procedures.

OBE implementation was characterized as involving a number of groundwork processes, including attitudinal and buy-in prerequisites, and the need for a facilitating staff development model for continued renewal. Frequently, the change is initiated through a core group, whose members serve as trainers and facilitators to each school. The current status of OBE was outlined and linked to Total Quality Management.

PRACTICAL EXERCISES

(1) Determine which structural or organizational elements, if any, in your district or school could be considered as containing some of the OBE concept.

(2) Assess how close a match your district's or school's delivery of program aimed at expected outcomes for students is to true mastery and outcome-based learning.

(3) Review the standards adopted by the Network for Outcome Based Schools, and assess the possibilities of each of them being acceptable to your school or district.

(4) Determine if there are academic requirements within the state or district curriculum that could be considered to be products, outputs, and outcomes.

(5) Estimate the types and amount of staff development that would be required for OBE implementation in your district.

REFERENCES

1. Spady, W. P. and K. J. Marshall. 1991. "Beyond Traditional Outcome-Based Education," *Educational Leadership,* 49(2):67–72.
2. Spady, W. G. 1988. "Organizing for Results: The Basis of Authentic Restructuring and Reform," *Educational Leadership,* 46(2):4–8.
3. Hobbs, M. E. and G. Bailey. 1987. "Outcome-Based Education Promises Higher Student Achievement and Less Stress for the Principal," *North Central Association Quarterly,* 61(3):406–411.
4. Spady, p. 5.
5. Friedland, S. 1992. "Building Student Self-Esteem for School Improvement," *NASSP Bulletin,* 76(540):96–102.
6. Rhodes, L. A. 1990. "Why Quality Is within Our Grasp . . . If We Reach," *School Administrator,* 47(10):31–34.
7. Herman, J. J. 1993. *Holistic Quality: Managing, Restructuring, Empowering Schools.* Newbury Park, CA: Corwin Press, Inc., a Sage Publications Company.
8. Spady, p. 5.
9. Schleisman, K. E. and J. A. King. 1990. "Making Sense of Outcome-Based Education: Where Did It Come from, and What Is It?" Research Report #7, Minneapolis, MN: Center for Applied Research and Educational Improvement.
10. Spady and Marshall, p. 67.
11. Spady, p. 7.
12. *Outcomes.* 1991. "Criteria for Outcome-Based Education," *Outcomes: A Quarterly Newsletter for the Network for Outcome Based Schools,* Johnson City, NY (Spring):5.
13. Spady, p. 7.
14. Kulieke, M. J. 1991. "Assessing Outcomes of Significance," *Outcomes: A Quarterly Newsletter of the Network for Outcome Based Schools,* Johnson City, NY (Winter):25–29.
15. Spady and Marshall, p. 70.
16. Rubin, S. E. and W. G. Spady. 1984. "Achieving Excellence through Outcome-Based Instructional Delivery," *Educational Leadership,* 41(8):37–44.
17. Fitzpatrick, K. A. 1991. "Restructuring to Achieve Outcomes of Significance for All Students: A Progress Report from Township High School District 214," *Outcomes: A Quarterly Newsletter of the Network for Outcome Based Schools,* Johnson City, NY (Winter):14–22.
18. Nyland, L. 1991. "One District's Journey to Success with Outcome-Based Education," *School Administrator,* 48(9):29, 31–32, 34–35.

19. King, J. A. and K. M. Evans. 1991. "Can We Achieve Outcome-Based Education?" *Educational Leadership,* 49(2):73–75.

20. Vickery, T. R. 1990. "ODDM: A Workable Model for Total School Improvement," *Educational Leadership,* 47(7):67–70.

21. Nyland, pp. 31–35.

22. Rubin and Spady, pp. 39–43.

23. Abrams, J. D. 1985. "Making Outcome-Based Education Work," *Educational Leadership,* 43(1):30–32.

24. Champlin, J. 1991. "A Powerful Tool for School Transformation," *School Administrator,* 48(9):34.

25. Rhodes, L. A. 1990. "Beyond Your Beliefs: Quantum Leaps Towards Quality Schools," *School Administrator,* 47(11):23–26.

26. Zlatos, B. 1993. "Outcomes-Based Outrage," *Executive Educator,* 15(9):12–16.

CHAPTER 7

School-Based Management: An Internal and External Customer Empowerment Structure for Educational Quality Management

THIS chapter discusses (1) defining School-Based Management (SBM); (2) deciding upon the structure and processes of SBM; (3) determining the categories and numbers of persons to be included on the SBM committees; (4) determining the decision areas of SBM; (5) determining which decisions are delegated to the building (site) level, which remain at the central district level, and which are to be shared by the building and central levels; (6) processing decisions; (7) methods of designing, collecting, and evaluating impact and effectiveness data related to SBM; (8) providing the training required to implement SBM; (9) developing policies to implement SBM; (10) developing operating by-laws within which to operate the SBM committees; (11) developing structures for SBM budgeting; (12) developing structures for SBM personnel decision making; (13) developing structures for SBM instructional decision making; (14) advantages and cautions of SBM; (15) enabling behaviors and bridges to new practice; and (16) a theory-to-practice example.

School-Based Management (SBM), sometimes called Site-Based Management, is a restructuring movement that is rapidly growing in strength among school districts across the United States [1]. Some state legislatures, such as those in Kentucky and Texas, have mandated SBM for every school district in their state [2]. In addition, many of the national professional educational associations have followed the lead of the American Association of School Administrators, the National Association of Elementary School Principals, and the National Association of Secondary School Principals in promoting SBM in the school districts across the nation [3].

SCHOOL-BASED MANAGEMENT DEFINED

An exploration of School-Based Management begins by defining the

73

term. Although various definitions exist, it is clear that School-Based Management involves the following:

- It is a dramatic change in both the structure and processes from the way that business has been traditionally conducted in school districts [4].
- It reallocates and redistributes traditional decision-making authority, in many areas, from the central district level to the individual school building level [5].
- It involves representatives of teachers and parents and the principal in making important site-based decisions. In some cases, it also includes students and community representatives in this decision-making structure [6].
- It allows the local SBM committees to make important site-related decisions in some or all of the areas of budget, personnel, instruction, policy, student services, and governance [7].

SBM STRUCTURES AND PROCESSES

Unless the structure and processes under which SBM operates are legislated, as is the case with the Kentucky Education Reform Act of 1990, each school district's decision makers who are held responsible for planning for the implementation and maintenance of SBM in their district must decide which stakeholders to involve in the SBM structure. In addition, they must negotiate and decide upon which decisions (and the degree to which final decision-making powers) are to be granted to the local school building level, which are to be retained by central school district functionaries, and which are to be shared by the building and central levels [8,9].

Once it has been decided that SBM is to be implemented in the school district, the first step is that of deciding which representatives of stakeholders' groups to involve in the SBM structure [10].

CATEGORIES AND NUMBERS OF PERSONS TO BE INCLUDED ON THE SBM COMMITTEES

Unless the structure and processes for SBM are legislated, as is the case in Kentucky and Texas, each school district's functionaries must decide which stakeholder groups are to be represented on the school building's SBM committees [11]. In addition, the local decision makers have to negotiate which decisions and the degree to which each decision is to be granted to, or divided between, the local school building and the central school district levels [12].

It is wise to assemble an SBM steering committee and to allow that steering committee to create as many subcommittees as the steering committee's membership deems useful to accomplish its work. In this manner, the steering committee membership can be kept to a reasonable size to allow it to operate efficiently and effectively, while the subcommittee structure allows the involvement of a large number of interested and important stakeholders [13,14].

Once the basic structural design is decided upon, the next step is to determine the categories of stakeholder representatives to be included. The membership options include: (1) the building principals; (2) teachers; (3) building-level classified employees; (4) one or more liaison members from the central school district office; (5) parents; (6) community members; (7) business, industrial, civic, and other governmental unit representatives; and (8) students (usually at a secondary school level) [15,16]. A description of the relative importance of including each of these categories of representation to the SBM committees follows:

(1) *The building principal,* research implies, is the most important figure in causing change and focus on quality education. However, this is true only when the principal is a leader as well as a manager, has a clear vision of what should be, is focused on quality educational achievement by each student and by all students, and has the ability to cause other important employees and stakeholders to claim ownership and to provide support to the SBM process.

(2) *Teachers* must be involved because they are the ones who deal directly with the students and are ultimately accountable for the progress of each child or youth entrusted to their supervision.

(3) *Classified employees* should be included in the membership of the SBM committee because many of them live in the community and have an important influence on community members' opinions about the quality of the school's programs.

(4) *A central office liaison* will be useful as a communications link between the central office and the local school building. This liaison, however, should only serve as an *ad hoc* member of the SBM committee.

(5) *Parents* definitely should be included in the SBM committee

membership, as they provide the children to educate and the taxes that allow the schools to exist. They are also the persons who probably have the greatest interest in and the most stake in the results of the schools.

(6) *Community members,* if feasible, should be included in the SBM steering committee membership. If the inclusion of community members would cause the SBM steering committee to become unwieldy in the number of members, it is wise to include them in important SBM subcommittees' membership.

(7) *Business, industrial, civic clubs, and other governmental unit representatives,* if feasible, should be included in SBM steering committee membership. If this is not feasible, then they should be included in important SBM subcommittees' membership.

(8) *Students* and the quality of their education are the most important reason for the existence of any school district or individual school. They are the products, and they will form the future citizenry who will become either productive or nonproductive members of our society. To enhance the quality of their education, they can be an important source of *what is* and *what should be* data [17,18].

In practically all SBM situations, teachers and the principal are included in membership. In many cases, parents are included in membership. Occasionally, community members, business representatives, industrial representatives, civic club, and nonschool governmental unit representatives are included. Very seldom are students and classified employees included in SBM committee membership. It is crucial that each school district and the individual school develop a broad-based and positive ownership of the SBM program, and it is also critical that the SBM committee be comprised of the broadest representative mix that is feasible [19]. For only by broad-based representation will true ownership of SBM evolve, and only through this broad representation will the probability of successfully initiating and maintaining SBM be maximized.

SBM DECISION AREAS

Once the structure of the SBM committee's membership has been decided upon, the local decision makers must turn to the areas and degrees of decision-making authority and responsibility to be delegated to the building level, to be retained at the central level, and to be shared by the building and central levels. The base decisions and the detailed subdecisions related to the areas of policy, budget, personnel, and instruction are crucial considerations, for the quality of these decisions will determine the probability of successful implementation and maintenance of SBM.

DECISIONS TO BE MADE AT THE BUILDING LEVEL OR CENTRAL DISTRICT LEVEL OR SHARED BETWEEN THE TWO LEVELS

Determination must be made by the central office authorities and the building-level decision makers related to which decisions can be made at each level and which decisions require collaborative input. Figure 7.1 presents a series of questions to be decided by the central-level and building-level decision makers.

Once the decision-making relationships have been determined in sufficient detail, it is very important to deal with the method of processing those decisions and with the training requirements of this group of individuals who comprise the SBM committee who have not necessarily worked together or who have not previously made decisions in the areas where decisions have been delegated to the building level. Without the clear processing of decisions and without sufficient training to enhance the probability of successful implementation of SBM, a predictable negative result will accrue. If the initial attempt fails, it will be many years before a second attempt to implement SBM will even be possible.

PROCESSING DECISIONS

If SBM is to work well, decisions should be made through consensus. Consensus, in this sense, is defined as all parties agreeing to the decision. If some members are not in favor of the decision made by the majority, but they indicate it is permissible to implement that decision, consensus has been reached. If, however, some members do not agree with the desire of the majority and they are not willing to allow the decision to be implemented, consensus has not been reached. This is a high standard; but if ownership is crucial to an excellent team approach, it is crucial that consensus be the method of choice [21].

Not only should the method of decision making be agreed upon, but

DIRECTIONS: place an "X" in the appropriate column indicating where the decision-making final authority rests. After making these base decisions, detail the action formats designed to smoothly carry out the decisions. These decisions relate to the detailed decision-making authority subsumed under the major categories of: (1) budget, (2) instruction, (3) personnel, and (4) policy.

	Building Level	Central Level	Joint Decision
Budget Area:			
1. Determine employee salaries, if merit pay			
2. Construct building budget			
3. Determine expenditures of building budget			
a. supplies			
b. equipment			
c. staff development			
d. co-curricular activities			
e. maintenance			
f. custodial services			
g. transportation			
h. food services			
i. other			
Instructional Area:			
1. Determine curriculum			
2. Determine instructional time schedule			
3. Determine subjects to be taught			
4. Determine instructional delivery methods			
5. Determine student assignments and grouping			
6. Determine testing and assessment procedures			
7. Determine student grading procedures			
8. Other			

Figure 7.1. An SBM interrogatory [20].

	Building Level	Central Level	Joint Decision
Personnel Area:			
1. Selection of teaching and classified staff			
2. Placement/assignment of teaching and classified staff			
3. Evaluation of teaching and classified staff			
4. Employment decisions related to tenure and dismissal of teaching and classified staff			
5. Selection of principal			
6. Placement assignment of principal			
7. Evaluation of principal			
8. Employment decisions related to the principal			
9. Other			
Policy Area:			
1. Can building policies be developed a. related to students b. related to employees c. related to other matters			
2. Can building policies differ with district policies			
3. Can the building obtain exemption from building policies for justified reasons			
4. Other			

Figure 7.1 (continued). An SBM interrogatory [20].

the means of arriving at decisions should be established. Some guidelines for processing include the following:

- Any member can initiate a topic or request investigation of a problem or a program desire.
- A method of investigating background information has to be determined.
- An analysis of the data collected has to be conducted.
- Alternative solutions should be discussed.

- Each solution should be carefully reviewed for its advantages, disadvantages, and "best fit."
- The preferred solution should be adopted by consensus of all members of the SBM committee or subcommittee.
- The preferred solution should be implemented, and plans should be made to evaluate the future effects of that decision.
- At a future point, an impact evaluation should be conducted; and a decision should be made to: (1) continue implementing the original decision, (2) modify and again implement the modified decision, or (3) drop the decided-upon action and initiate an alternate action.

METHODS OF DESIGNING, COLLECTING, AND EVALUATING IMPACT AND EFFECTIVENESS DATA RELATED TO SBM

Once the SBM committee and its subcommittees are certain of their roles and decision-making areas and the membership has received the necessary prerequisite training, the SBM committee is ready to go to work. Its initial task is to arrive at a needs assessment. A need is a gap or discrepancy between what currently exists and what should or could be in the future [22].

Needs can be assessed from: (1) identified problems to be solved, (2) program enhancements that are desired, or (3) any other important matter which identifies the gap between what exists and what should or could exist at some future point. Needs may be of the mega (societal), macro (total organization) and/or micro (subunit) category. For example, two mega needs may be those of allowing community use of the school building after normal school hours or providing continuous information about the goals and accomplishments of the school's students and employees.

A macro need may be to develop a belief system in which all employees truly realize that *all* students can learn. A micro need could well be one of reducing the dropout rate and absenteeism rates in grades eleven and twelve at a specific high school.

Once the information has been collected to provide a comprehensive needs assessment, the SBM committee and its subcommittees must identify what they believe is the *preferred future vision,* in all of its dimensions, for the school. Once this preferred future vision has been agreed upon, the SBM committee has to sell this vision to all of the constituent stakeholders of the school; and it must arrive at action plans to address the identified needs in a way that these plans will ultimately achieve, or, at least, more closely approach, the preferred future vision [23].

SBM TRAINING REQUIRED

When a group of individuals such as principals, teachers, parents, and community members are brought together in an SBM committee structure, they are not an immediately effective working and decision-making group. Also, when the members of an SBM committee are suddenly empowered to make decisions in areas where they have never previously had decision-making power, some training of the membership must be built into the process. In addition, training must be provided on a continual basis, since membership will change over time [24].

Each SBM building-level committee and/or subcommittee will have specific and individualized training needs, and these will have to be determined at the local building level. However, there is a commonality of training requirements that will, in all probability, apply to every SBM committee and/or subcommittee regardless of which school building or which school district is involved in School-Based Management. The main common training needs [25,26] are:

- team building
- verbal and nonverbal communication
- problem or program identification
- information collection techniques
- information analysis techniques
- collaborative decision-making procedures
- strategic and tactical planning methods, which include the development of a preferred future vision for the school, a mission statement, and action plans
- development of policy statements, policy analyses, and standard operating procedures
- change agentry
- marketing, selling, presenting, and public relations
- leadership and followership

- definition of desired results and the means of measuring the degree of achievement of the desired results

Obviously, all of these training needs must be addressed over a long time period, but this should not be a concern, since SBM at the building level is not a *quick fix*. Rather, it is an evolutionary process. The most immediate training needs are those of communication, problem identification and solution, team building, and planning methods.

Once the training schedule has been decided upon, it is important to turn to the methods of designing, collecting, and evaluating the impact and effectiveness data related to SBM.

POLICIES TO IMPLEMENT SBM

Policies are general directional statements of intent that are formally adopted by a board of education at legally scheduled meetings. It is important that the official representative body of the district display its support for the SBM approach by formally adopting policy statements that are supportive of this approach [27].

Board of education policies should include such statements as the following:

- Wonderful School District's Board of Education favors the School-Based Management approach to decision making, as it realizes that many of the decisions made in the district related to the effectiveness and efficiency of the local school's operation are more effectively and efficiently made by a representative group of stakeholders who are provided decision-making power over many of the decisions related to: (1) instruction, (2) budget, (3) personnel, and (4) school building governance issues.
- Wonderful School District's Board of Education directs the superintendent of schools to organize a planning committee for the purpose of initiating a School-Based Management program within one year and to allocate the resources necessary to accomplish this task.

OPERATIONAL BY-LAWS FOR SBM COMMITTEES

With the official support of the board of education assured, the SBM planners must develop the detailed by-laws required to allow the local school building committees to operate with full knowledge of their structure, their responsibilities, and the processes they are to utilize. The main decisions to be incorporated into the operational by-laws should include the following elements [28]:

- deciding on who is to be represented on the SBM steering committee, how the members are to selected, how long each member is to serve, and the parameters of their decision-making authority and accountability
- decision making to be made by the consensus method
- relief from existing board of education policies available by request when the local SBM committee feels that the district policy is negatively affecting what is happening at the school level
- authority to create subcommittees and to define each subcommittee's duties and responsibilities

SBM BUDGETING STRUCTURES AND PROCESSES

Each district must reach negotiating decisions on the roles of the local SBM committee and the central office functionaries related to budgeting. One method that is easily administered is to allow a definite amount of dollars to be allocated to the local school building SBM committee for their use in any manner that the SBM committee feels is in the best interest of their local school's children and their educational environment. A standard dollar amount can be allocated per student, or per teacher, or by some other standard procedure. These standards can also be weighted, if desired, by allowing varying amounts by grade level, by handicapped students, by gifted students, by vocational students, or by music, art, physical education or any other consideration that the local SBM committee and the school district's officials determine to be reasonable.

SBM PERSONNEL STRUCTURES AND PROCESSES

Again, the decisions related to personnel will have to be negotiated by the local school's and the school district's decision makers. One method is to allow a weighting system using 100 employee teacher equivalency per 1,000 students. For example, a school of 500 students would be authorized to employ 50 teacher equivalencies.

The number of personnel hired could be determined, then, by agreeing on different weightings for various personnel. For example, a principal could be weighted as 2.00, assistant principal at 1.75, a teacher at 1.00, a teacher aide at .60, a twelve-month secretary at .75, and a nine-month secretary at .55 equivalency. This model assumes that custodial, maintenance, food service, and transportation personnel will be controlled by the central office. In this model, the local SBM committee could decide how to hire a principal and how to determine the numbers of assistant principals, teachers, teacher aides, and secretaries to be hired for the local school building.

The process used to select and hire employees could be shared between the central office and the local SBM committee in a way that prevents any level from selecting an employee who is not also agreeable to the other level. The central office could recruit candidates; representatives from both the building and central level could determine which candidates should be brought in for interviews; and the SBM committee can be given final selection recommendation authority. Obviously, the board of education cannot delegate its final legal decision-making authority; but, for all practical purposes, the final hiring decision could be left with the local school's SBM committee.

SBM INSTRUCTIONAL STRUCTURES AND PROCESSES

Again, the district's and local school building's decision makers will have to develop their own negotiated sharing of power in this area. A logical structure could well be that of a committee comprised of six (or some other number) teachers; a principal; a central office instructional specialist; six members of an SBM subcommittee; six secondary students; and an agreed-upon number of consultants and/or community, business, industrial, civic, or nonschool governmental representatives if these additions are deemed to add knowledge and support to the task [29].

ADVANTAGES AND CAUTIONS RELATED TO SBM

If done well, School-Based Management should result in some or all of the following indicators: (1) the achievements of students and employees should increase; (2) the organizational climate should improve and become a more creative and caring one; (3) parent and community support should increase; (4) the school(s) should become results-oriented rather than means-oriented; (5) the culture should become one of effectiveness and efficiency; (6) wide student, employee, parental, and community ownership of both the services and products should be evidenced; (7) strategic and tactical planning should be considered crucial, and there should be consistent monitoring, feedback, and evaluation of every decision and program; (8) communication to all groups should become two-way, continuous, and positive; (9) a wide variety and number of stakeholders should have opportunities for input, and they will feel ownership of the vision, mission, decisions, programs, and products of the school(s) [30].

As is true of any major restructuring within a school district, SBM will initiate a dramatic change in structure, procedures, and involvement. Since change is difficult at best, and since change that ultimately modifies the culture of an organization and its standard operating procedures is doubly difficult for people to accept and adjust to, it is crucial that much attention be placed on the human element. Therefore, there is only one major potential disadvantage of implementing SBM. *If the decision makers do not attend to the human elements when making the change to SBM structure and processes, it will be doomed to failure.* In addition, if the initial attempt fails, it will be next to impossible to again introduce SBM or any other major change in the immediate or intermediate future.

ENABLING BEHAVIORS AND BRIDGES TO NEW PRACTICE

It is clear that the educators who are to implement School-Based Management must be recruited with a careful eye toward the skills, knowledge, and attitudes implied throughout this chapter as requirements for such successful implementation. Also, it is clear that university training must inculeate the future educators in these skills, knowledge, and attitudes, through both academic courses and field-based experiences. The literature and publications focused on School-Based Management have shown that some training and preparation programs will need to be focused exclusively on administrators, but a substantial portion might be more appropriately provided to administrator/teacher teams. Training should, indeed, reflect the work of the school and include problem-centered materials. A broad and continuing training program for all members of the school community, including school board members and central office staff, should reflect the program integration required by the interdependency of the individuals in a school-based environment.

Some of the elements in getting a group of employees, students, and community members to support dramatic changes and to create a viable SBM structure involve the following:

- An individual leader or a group of stakeholders must conceptualize a vision of what the schools are to look like at some future point in time.
- A critical mass of stakeholders who are going to be called upon to be involved in envisioning what the schools are to look like in the future must be made aware of the new vision and of the changes that will be required to achieve that vision, and they should be given an opportunity to provide feedback.
- Whenever possible, this feedback should be used to make necessary or desired changes in the original vision.
- Activities must be decided upon and activated to implement the required changes, and people have to be motivated to act in the directions of the desired changes.
- A system must be inaugurated and maintained to collect data, to provide support for those implementing the change, and to provide the necessary skill training for those implementers who do not possess the necessary skills.
- Finally, a system of recognition of individuals and groups who contribute to the desired change direction should be maintained, and celebrations should be held whenever a milestone is reached.

THEORY-TO-PRACTICE EXAMPLE

The hypothetical Exceptional Senior High School in the hypothetical Excellent School District will be utilized to briefly illustrate the structure and processes used by a school entering into an SBM restructuring model. The points of interest will be identified, and a brief discussion of each point will be presented.

Deciding on the SBM Committee Structure and Required Operational Process

It is decided that there will be a building-level steering committee made up of representatives of teachers, classified employees, parents, and the principal. Except for the principal, the initial appointment will be one year for one-third of each representative group, two years for one-third of each group, and three years for one-third of each group. Following the initial appointments, all future appointments will be for three years, with one-third of the SBM membership changing each year. It was also agreed that any individual could serve additional terms if they were elected by their referent group.

It was decided that the steering committee would consist of eighteen members, with six being elected by each referent group; and the principal would become the nineteenth member of the SBM steering committee. In addition, it was agreed that the steering committee could appoint subcommittees, at any time, for a specific purpose and for a specific time period. Finally, it was decided that the committee membership should elect a chairperson from its members, and it could elect any other functionaries that the committee members felt necessary to carry on its business effectively and efficiently.

It was also decided that all steering committee and subcommittee meetings will be publicized in advance and that all meetings will be open to anyone who wishes to observe the committee's deliberations. Finally, it was decided that all decisions reached would be by the consensus method. All of these matters were placed in a written set of bylaws designed to govern the committee's functioning.

Deciding upon the Decisions that are Delegated to the Building Level, that are Retained by the Central Level, and that are to Be Shared Decisions

In the area of instruction, it was decided that the local SBM committee could develop the curriculum guides, select the instructional materials, and determine the instructional delivery methods used. However, it was agreed that the courses offered and the time sequence of the instructional schedule will be determined by the central office unless the Exceptional High School's SBM committee requests and receives a waiver from the central office administration.

In the area of budget, it was decided that the local school would be given a standardized weighted dollar budgeted amount per student of $250, and this amount could be expended totally at the discretion of the local school district's SBM committee. It was agreed that the costs associated with custodial, maintenance, food services, co-curricular activities, and transportation services will be budgeted for and expended from the central office budget.

Additionally, it was decided that the local school will be provided $550 per teacher, $225 per classified employee, and $225 per SBM committee member for staff development and training. This amount was to be totally expended at the discretion of the SBM committee.

In the area of personnel, the SBM committee was given total authority to select the teachers and classified employees for their school building, but the principal was to agree with the committee's choice. Also, the SBM committee was to agree with the principal's choice. All placements, transfers, evaluations, or dismissals of any employees, however, were determined to be solely in the hands of the principal, central office director of personnel, and the superintendent of schools.

If a principal vacancy occurs, the central office is to assist the SBM committee in recruiting candidates. The committee, however, shall be free to recommend their choice for principal, but the superintendent of schools will have to agree to that selection. On the other hand, it was decided that the superintendent of schools was not permitted to select a principal whom the committee does not find acceptable.

The evaluation, or dismissal, of any principal is to be solely in the hands of the central office director of personnel and the superintendent of schools.

In the area of governance, the SBM committee is permitted to develop a complete set of policies to govern the operations of their schools. The committee was not allowed to adopt a policy that was in conflict with a school district–level policy, but the committee could ask for an exemption from any district-level policy.

Developing a Schedule for the Training of SBM Committee Members

A continuous schedule of training for the SBM committee members was developed. Within the first three months of operation, the training focused on communications skills, team building, and identification of needs. Throughout the year, training continued on many areas of strategic and tactical planning methodologies, information retrieval strategies, marketing and selling, presenting, and numerous other training areas as identified by the committee members. As members would be changing over time, it was decided to establish separate training sessions for the new members; and the experienced members were to be involved as part of the training staff.

Conducting a Needs Assessment and Arriving at a Preferred Future Vision

The committee identified needs by looking at the role the school should play in society (mega needs), by looking at the needs for the total school building (macro needs), and by identifying the needs of the various subjects and co-curricular programs offered by the school (micro needs). One example of each type of need identified by Exceptional High School's SBM Committee will illustrate what this need assessment approach revealed.

- It was discovered that the parents, students, and community members felt that there was very little understanding by the high school students of the necessity of being part of a caring and assisting group of community residents. It was decided that an action plan had to be initiated to assist in meeting this identified need. This is an example of a mega need.
- There was a general problem with student vandalism with the school's building and grounds. Because of the poor image being displayed to the community and because of the unnecessary cost of repairing the vandalism, it was decided to quickly put into place an action program to solve this macro need.
- A micro need that was identified was that of poor academic achievement by students identified as at-risk students. It was agreed that action programs must be developed to attempt to meet this need.

Developing Action Plans Designed to Achieve the Preferred Future Vision and to Eliminate the Identified Needs

Using the same needs—a mega need to develop a sense of community service responsibility among all students, a macro need to stop student vandalism, and the micro need to assist in raising the academic achievement level of those students identified as being at risk—it is now possible to indicate the action plans undertaken by the SBM committee. To address the mega need for community service, the SBM committee presented a proposal to the board of education that required each freshman student to complete a one credit hour of community service; and each senior would have to complete another hour of community service before she/he could receive a diploma and graduate from Exceptional High School. Such activities as driving elderly people to stores or doctors, assisting in painting houses of persons who could not afford to maintain their homes, and a variety of other community services, equivalent to a minimum of 100 hours of service, had to be provided by each student.

To address the macro need to stop vandalism, the SBM committee instituted an incentive approach. The staff, at the request of the SBM committee, provided a recreation area for student use prior to school opening, during lunch hour, and after school hours; and the students could decorate and equip it to their liking. However, the students were to be held responsible for the cleanliness and maintenance of that area; and the privilege of the student recreation area was to exist only if the record of vandalism was eliminated or greatly reduced. In addition, the equivalent of the amount of money previously expended to repair the acts of vandalism was given to a student governing committee to be spent for equipment or decorations for their recreation area.

To address the micro need to improve the academic achievement of students identified as being at risk, the staff, with the assistance of the teachers, took a dual action approach. First, they instituted a cooperative learning structure, where students of all levels of achievement worked together to study and complete project assignments. Second, teachers and parent volunteers provided an after-school study program and a phone-in homework help line to assist the at-risk students.

Monitoring, Collecting Data, and Evaluating the Impact and Effectiveness of the Action Plans and the SBM Structure and Processes

Not only did the SBM committee identify the needs and develop action program proposals, they also established, with the assistance of the administrators and teachers, an information gathering, monitoring, and assessment of results system. Prior to initiating any of the action programs, facts were gathered to establish baseline data. These data indicated the attitudes of students toward community service, the yearly cost pattern of vandalism, the numbers of at-risk students, and the degree to which each was academically underachieving.

After the students had served their required community service, a combination of interviews with students and the completion of an attitudinal survey by all student participants indicated that there was a great increase in the students' positive view of community service. The level of change in attitude was such that the program was put into place as a standard graduation requirement.

Using the initial district expenditure records and comparable records for the one-year period after the students were provided with their recreational area, it was possible to determine that the vandalism decreased by 93%. The allocation of a space for students to develop their own recreation area and the provision of money saved from vandalism clean-up for student use in their recreation area proved to be an effective action program.

In attempting to solve the underachievement of students identified as being at risk, mixed results were discovered. When the norm-referenced standardized test results and the criterion-referenced test results from the current year were compared to those of prior years, it was found that only 60% of the at-risk students gained an expected amount of academic achievement. On further analysis, it was found that most of the 60% of the students who displayed satisfactory achievement growth were those who participated in cooperative learning opportunities, who frequently took advantage of the after-school tutorial help, and who also frequently took advantage of the students' homework assistance phone service. The SBM committee felt a commitment, at its next meeting, to try to identify other action programs that would assist the 40% of the at-risk students who were not benefiting from the original action program approaches.

Celebrating Successes and Recycling the Entire Process

As is illustrated by the fact that 40% of the at-risk students were not reached by the initial action programs attempted, it is important that the SBM committee members do not get discouraged and that they immediately go back to the drawing board to develop a modified or different program to attempt to meet the identified need. It is important that all failures are seen as learning activities that will lead to future improvement.

It is equally important for the committee members to celebrate each success, and they should broadcast their successes throughout the school and throughout the community at large. Success begets success, but it only leads to pride and ownership if it is celebrated and publicized.

CONCLUSION

Key SBM concepts are relatively few in number, but they provide powerful directional changes in the traditional ways school districts are operated. These key concepts include the following:

- Traditional central district decision making will be modified in such a manner that many or all decisions related to instruction, budget, personnel, and governance will be relegated to the individual school building (site) level.
- Persons who have not been traditionally empowered to make decisions that were made by central functionaries are now empowered to make decisions related to their school building's structure and processes. Membership on SBM committees always include the building principal and the teachers within that building. Many times, parents will be included in the membership of the school's SBM committee; and, occasionally, students, classified staff, and community representatives are included in the SBM committee's membership.
- Collaborative decision making is the trademark of all SBM operations.
- Planning skills are required to successfully implement and maintain the SBM operation.
- A climate conducive of support for the school district's and individual school's programs and procedures will exist in those districts and schools who successfully implement SBM.

SUMMARY

This chapter has defined School-Based Management as a common restructuring movement and a change process that reallocates and redistributes budgetary, personnel, instructional, and policy decision-making authority to a stakeholder-representative group. It was recommended that an SBM steering committee be established to create subcommittees and that the local decision makers determine the division of governance between the local buildings and the central levels.

Likewise, it indicated that the SBM decision-making committee membership configuration should be determined; stakeholders usually include principals and teachers; other representatives may include classified employees, central office personnel, parents (strongly recommended), community and business members, and (secondary) students. The determination of decisions to be made at the building level or at the central level, or to be shared, is critical. An interrogatory addressing this need was provided. The processing of those decisions and the training requirements for the SBM committee members were discussed. Decision process rules and the ability to achieve consensus are critical procedures and skills for the SBM committee.

The committee's initial task was described as one of applying the strategic planning needs assessment process in order to develop action plans to address the preferred future vision. Essential training requirements for such committee action included team building, communication, preplanning strategies, and collaborative decision-making procedures. An example of SBM budgetary structures and process was given, describing a standard per student dollar allocation. Similarly, personnel and instructional examples suggested a weighted system for assigning personnel in standard teacher units per building, and a suggestion for the negotiation of shared curricular power was presented. A description of the advantages and cautions of SBM preceded a listing of the training and staff development prerequisites needed to facilitate successful implementation. A theory-to-practice example of implementation of restructuring a hypothetical high school was included.

PRACTICAL EXERCISES

(1) Which of the described combined SBM reform elements do you feel will be the most enduring and why?

(2) Which of the elements required to support dramatic systematic change do you think are the most achievable in your district?

(3) Compare the quality of your professional preparation with that described as needed for SBM leadership and implementation. What elements are already present and which ones would need further training?

(4) Reflect and estimate the possibility, in your district and on a national scale, of achieving that balance of shared decision making that is the hallmark of School-Based Management.

REFERENCES

1. Herman, J. J. 1990. "School-Based Management," *Instructional Leader* (journal of the Texas Elementary and Supervisors Association), 3(4):1–5.

2. Herman, J. J. and J. L. Herman. 1992. *School-Based Management: Current Thinking and Practice*. Springfield, IL: Charles C. Thomas, Publisher.

3. Herman, J. L. and J. J. Herman. 1993. "A State by State Snapshot of School-Based Management Practices," *International Journal of Educational Reform*, 2(3):256–262.

4. Hill, P. T., J. J. Bonan and K. Warner. 1992. "Uplifting Education," *National School Board Journal*, 179(3):21–25.

5. Herman, J. J. 1989. "A Decision-Making Model: Site-Based Communications Governance Committees," *NASSP Bulletin*, 73(521):61–66.

6. Hall, G. E. and S. M. Hord. 1987. *Change in Schools: Facilitating the Process*. Albany, NY: State University of New York Press, p. 51.

7. Herman, J. J. 1992. "Key Steps to Develop School Governance Teams," *The School Administrator*, 49(1):34–35.

8. Lane, J. and E. Epps (eds.). 1992. *Restructuring the Schools: Problems and Prospects*. Berkeley, CA: McCutchan Publishing Corporation.

9. Herman, J. J. and J. L. Herman. 1991. *The Positive Development of Human Resources and School District Organizations*. Lancaster, PA: Technomic Publishing Company, Inc., pp. 19–20.

10. Herman, J. J. 1992. "School-Based Management: Sharing the Resource Decisions," *NASSP Bulletin*, 76(545):102–105.

11. Herman, J. J. 1993. "School-Based Management," *Educational Facilities Planner*, 31(1):30.

12. Herman, J. J. and G. Megiveron. 1993. *Collective Bargaining in Education: Win/Win, Win/Lose, Lose/Lose*. Lancaster, PA: Technomic Publishing Company, Inc.

13. Schiller, R. E. and C. W. Freed. 1992. "Who Will Be at the Leadership Helm in the 1990's?" *The School Administrator*, 49(3):46–47.

14. Lewis, J., Jr. 1989. *Implementing School-Based Management by Empowering Teachers*. Westbury, NY: J. L. Wilkerson Publishing Co.

15. NASSP. 1991. *School-Based Management: Theory and Practice*. Reston, VA: National Association of Secondary School Principals.

16. Herman, J. J. 1990. "School Based Management: A Checklist of Things to Consider," *NASSP Bulletin*, 74(527):67–71.

17. Herman, J. J. 1993. *Holistic Quality: Managing, Restructuring, Empowering Schools*. Newbury Park, CA: Corwin Press, Inc., a Sage Publications Company.

18. Schlechty, P. C. 1990. *Schools for the Twenty-First Century*. San Francisco, CA: Jossey-Bass Publishers, pp. 145–146.

19. Herman, J. J. and J. L. Herman. 1992. "Educational Administration: School-Based Management," *The Clearing House*, 65(5):261–263.

20. Herman, J. J. 1992. "School-Based Management: Staffing and Budget Expenditures," *School Business Affairs*, 58(12):24–25.

21. Herman, J. J. and J. L. Herman. In press. *Making Change Happen*. Newbury Park, CA: Corwin Press, Inc., a Sage Publications Company.

22. Herman, J. J. 1989. "Site-Based Management: Creating a Vision and Mission Statement," *NASSP Bulletin,* 73(519):79–83.

23. Herman, J. J. 1991. "School-Based Management: An Introduction," *School-Based Management: Theory and Practice.* Reston, VA: National Association of Secondary Principals, pp. v–vii.

24. Boyd, W. L. 1990. "Balancing Control and Autonomy in School Reform: The Politics of Perestroika," in *The Educational Reform Movement of the 1980's,* J. Murphy (ed.), Berkeley, CA: McCutchan Publishing Corporation, pp. 88–89, 94.

25. Herman and Megiveron. 1993. pp. 16–19.

26. Mojkowski, C. 1991. *Developing Leaders for Restructuring Schools: New Habits of Mind and Heart.* Washington, DC: National LEADership Network Study Group on Restructuring Schools, p. 49.

27. David, J. L. 1989. "Synthesis of Research on School-Based Management," *Educational Leadership,* 46(8):45–53.

28. Herman, J. J. and J. L. Herman. 1991. "Business Officials and School-Based Management," *School Business Affairs,* 57(11):34–37.

29. Barth, R. 1990. *Improving Schools from Within.* San Francisco, CA: Jossey-Bass Publishers, p. 145.

30. Herman, J. J. 1989. "Strategic Planner: One of the Changing Leadership Roles of the Principal," *The Clearing House,* 63(2):56–58.

CHAPTER 8

Educational Quality Management Basics: A Systematic Framework for Quality Schools

THIS chapter presents (1) a definition of Quality Management (QM), (2) a QM planning model structure, (3) requirements for the management of QM, (4) measurement of the results and evaluation of QM, (5) advantages and cautions related to QM, (6) key QM concepts, (7) enabling behaviors and bridges to new practice, and (8) a theory-to-practice example.

Various authors use terms such as Total Quality Management, Quality Process, or simply Quality to write about the area of quality in organizations. Indeed, there appears to be no single definition for this movement. Although there is no uniform definition, there are definite elements that appear in practically every quality movement discussion.

QUALITY MANAGEMENT DEFINED

- It is a *philosophy* that states that all products and services can and must continually be improved.
- It is a *goal* that identifies each milestone leading to the delivery of each product or service to internal and external customers, and it progressively improves them in order that the final product or service delivered is of the highest quality possible. This approach will ultimately lead to very satisfied customers.
- It is a process that obtains and uses feedback from a wide variety of customers to develop quality specifications for the organization's products and services, and it is a process that empowers and trains all employees to assist in improving quality at each value-added step of the development of each product of service ultimately delivered [1–3].

The message for each school and school district is to obtain continual feedback from both internal and external customers and to utilize all employees in the quest of the best possible quality of each product and service delivered to the school's or school district's customers [4]. To do otherwise is to be insensitive to customers' needs and desires and to neglect the value of empowering all employees in an effort to improve all products and services.

QM PLANNING MODEL STRUCTURE

In order to successfully implement and maintain Quality Management in a school district and/or its component schools, it is crucial that a comprehensive planning model be devised and used. Figure 8.1 illustrates such a planning model.

The first requirement for a school district to initiate Quality Management is that of educating the key decision makers about QM and then getting a positive go-ahead signal from the board of education, school administration, and a critical mass of stakeholders [5]. Only as key decision makers possess a good understanding of what is involved in QM and of the potential positive results that can be achieved by implementing QM can ownership be broadened to the degree necessary to predict successful implementation [6].

A second requirement for the successful implementation of QM is that of conducting a comprehensive needs assessment. This needs assessment should involve the employees, the internal student customers, and the external community customers. Customers are those individuals and groups that must perceive the products and services of the schools as being of high quality. A needs assessment of each of these categories of people involves the collection of significant hard data (such as student achievement scores) and significant soft data (such as opinion and/or attitude surveys). A comprehensive needs assessment also directs its investigation to three levels of needs (gaps between what is and what should be or what could be). The three levels consist of mega needs (those which the schools share with society), macro needs (those which involve the entire school district), and micro needs (those which involve individual schools or some other sub-element of a school or school district).

Once a comprehensive needs assessment has been completed, it is important that *strategic goals* be established for each of the mega, macro, and micro categories of needs. These strategic goals can then be used by the planners to develop *quality specifications* (specific

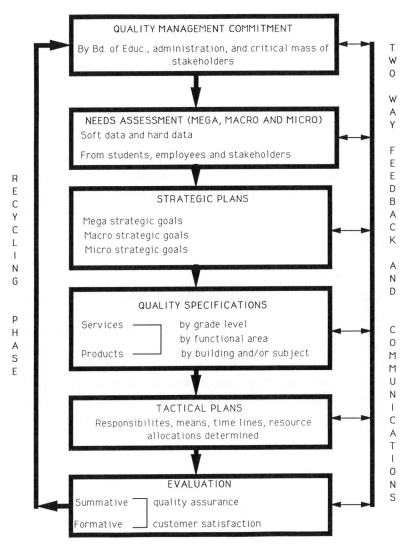

Figure 8.1. Quality Management model for school districts.

measurable objectives) for each of the services and products to be delivered by the school district and its constituent schools [7].

Once the planning stakeholders have developed the quality specifications, those responsible for tactical planning have to develop the means, ways, or programs designed to achieve the quality specifications agreed upon by the strategic planning stakeholders [8]. This tactical planning stage of implementation of QM involves deciding on the specific programs to be attempted in order to achieve the desired quality specifications and the strategic goals that are to be addressed. This stage of planning includes (1) deciding on each task to be completed and the chronological sequence for completion of each task to be included as a part of each action program, (2) determining which person or group is responsible for completing each task, (3) establishing timelines for each task to be completed, and (4) determining the resource allocations to be provided for the accomplishment of each task. Once the action plan is initiated, formative evaluative data are collected and analyzed for use in making decisions; and once the action program is completed, summative data is collected to determine the degree to which the program assisted in reaching the qualitative level of results spelled out in the initial quality specifications [9,10].

MANAGEMENT REQUIREMENTS OF QM

Once tactical planning is completed, the responsibility for the effectiveness of QM is passed to managers who are to make the action plans work well. Creating an overall quality culture is most important, but it is also important that those persons who are to manage the QM program on an ongoing basis fulfill the promise of QM by making sure that each milestone and each subtask is done in the highest quality manner possible.

These QM managers must assume an important leadership role by performing the following responsibilities:

- They must instill ownership of the QM culture in each employee, one that insists on improving the quality of each product and service.
- They have to make every employee feel that she/he is an important and integral part of the decision-making and delivery system of every product and service with which they are involved.
- They arrange for and fully utilize feedback from customers and measurements of quality, and they provide this data to each pertinent employee for that employee's use in improving each value-added step in the development of the product or service with which the employee is involved [11,12].

MEASUREMENT OF RESULTS AND EVALUATION OF QM

In order to evaluate the impact of the QM program and the products and services provided by the organization, formative and summative evaluations must be included as integral processes Formative evaluation data provide important information at each step of the delivery system, and these data can be used to determine whether or not the value-added quality targets are being met. If the value-added quality targets are not met, new intervention techniques can be applied to improve the quality of the service and/or product.

Summative evaluation data provide information at the end of a predetermined period of time; and these data can be used to modify, to eliminate, or to continue strengthening the processes in place that are designed to meet the two goals of continually improving the quality of each product and service. Summative evaluations, coupled with formative evaluations, ensure that the impact standards will either be met or that the product or service delivery processes will be modified to ensure that the impact standards will be ultimately met [13].

ADVANTAGES AND CAUTIONS RELATED TO QM

There are only two major cautions related to initiating and maintaining a successful Quality Management program. They are: (1) a critical mass of decision makers (board of education, administration, employees, customers) have to be knowledgeable about and buy into QM prior to implementation or it will not be successfully introduced or implemented; and (2) there' must be a culture, structure, and processes in place that have employees continually striving to improve all services and products.

Numerous advantages accrue to school districts and to the component schools that successfully implement Quality Management. The major advantages are as follows [14]:

- It focuses management, employees, and customers on the quest to produce the highest quality services and products possible.
- It focuses on improving each milestone's quality, rather than merely being satisfied with some improvement on the ultimately delivered service or product.

- It uses a continuing data collection and feedback system to focus on each step of the service or product to be delivered.
- It enlists the employees and the school district's or school's customers in providing feedback that assists in developing the quality specifications for which to strive.
- It uses formative and summative evaluations to determine the quality impact of each service and each product.

KEY QM CONCEPTS

Although there are many detailed tasks that must be accomplished to successfully implement QM in school districts and in individual schools, it is important to emphasize the underlying principles or concepts that exist if this structure and process-oriented restructuring method is to be attempted. The main QM concept are as follows [15–17]:

- It deals with quality goals, and it focuses on quality results in both the product and service areas.
- It deals with a *value-added* concept of quality at each juncture and over a continuing time frame.
- It empowers important stakeholders to make decisions that are designed to improve the quality of both products and services, and it provides the required training to ensure the capability of those empowered to achieve the quality mission.
- It stresses factual data collection and feedback based upon these data to all involved in managing the QM activities.
- It stresses customer satisfaction.
- It relies on planning to achieve the vision of total quality in all aspects of the organization's activities, products, services, and culture.

ENABLING BEHAVIORS AND BRIDGES TO NEW PRACTICE

Many of the previously described enabling behaviors and suggested staff development and training components listed in the preceding chapters are foundational to the application of Total Quality Management (TQM) in educational organizations, particularly in the planning function [18]. Actual preparatory steps consist primarily of the fostering of such attitudes and prerequisites as the following:

- The school district's and individual school's mission must focus on a vision, policies, and strategic goals that lead to the delivery of high-quality services and products to all customers.
- Educational customers include all internal (students and employees) and all external (parents, residents, and other agencies that interact with the schools) stakeholders.
- TQM should focus on the processes that are designed to continuously produce quality products at each step and to all customers.
- TQM has a value-added dimension, in that every step of the process will lead to an improved output; and quality is added to each step.
- Ultimately, customers define quality standards; and satisfaction of customers is only gained through meeting or exceeding these standards.
- Extensive two-way communications with all stakeholders are required to define the quality specifications to be used by the schools or school districts.
- TQM involves a systems approach, and TQM school districts' or school buildings' decision makers should constantly improve the quality of their systems or processes.
- Employees are empowered through communication, training, and encouraging leadership. Many times, problem-solving teams are utilized to remove glitches in the systems or processes [19,20].
- Training is continuously required for management, employees and suppliers to make certain that they are constantly attentive to improvement in the quality of the products and services.
- Constancy of measurement, not just limited to standardized test scores, is crucial to quality assurance.
- TQM is about change, and change involves causing changes in behaviors.
- School districts and schools that implement TQM must realize that it will cause changes and that these changes could be so dramatic that they ultimately change the culture of the school districts and schools that comprise them.

- In order to maintain this desired cultural state, school districts and schools will have to scan the external and internal environments to assess the potential impacts of internal and external variables that continuously keep changing. This must be done in order to effectively develop strategic and tactical plans to deal with these variables.
- In order for TQM to be seriously considered, transformational leadership must be present. Transformational leaders are those individuals who are visionaries that are driven by long-term goals to achieve the *preferred future quality vision* for their schools and school districts.
- TQM school districts and individual school buildings possess an environment—a learning climate—that emanates from a culture that speaks directly and constantly to the issue of quality. If this does not take place, the hoped-for quality school district or school building will become next year's major failure. If successfully done, quality will permeate every nook and cranny, as well as the thoughts of every stakeholder within the schools or the thoughts of those who have direct dealings with the schools.

THEORY-TO-PRACTICE EXAMPLE

Value-Added School District's activities related to its implementation and maintenance of Quality Management, for the sake of brevity, will be illustrated by brief descriptions and enhanced by a series of depictions of each activity's approach. The areas presented include (1) an employeee subsystem, (2) a student subsystem, (3) and external environment subsystem, (4) a strategic planning process subsystem, and (5) a tactical planning process subsystem [21].

Employee Subsystem

In order to successfully implement and maintain QM, it is absolutely crucial that the employees are able to deliver the products and services to meet the quality assurance specifications desired (see Figure 8.2). To begin, it is absolutely necessary to obtain and retain employees who believe in the organization's quality culture and in collaborative efforts to produce quality, to be dedicated to customers' satisfaction, and to continually attempt to improve the quality of services and products pro-

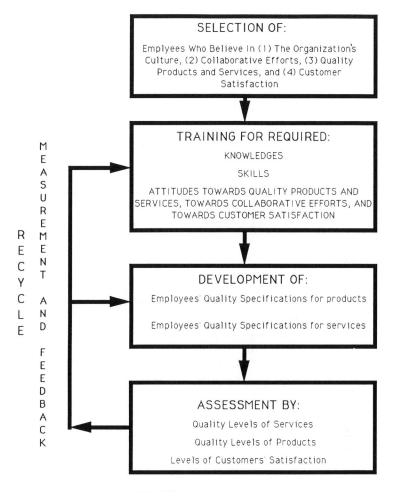

Figure 8.2. QM employee subsystem.

duced and delivered. Once the desired type of employees are in place and they possess the desired attitudes, it is crucial that the employees are trained in the knowledge and skills necessary to produce the desired quality of products and services. Also, with collaborative planning as the mode of operation, it is important to have the employees continuously assist in the development of the qaulity specifications. Finally, the employees must assist in assessing the (1) quality of the products delivered, (2) quality of the services delivered, and (3) degree of customers' satisfaction with those services and products [22].

Student Subsystem

Once the appropriate employees are hired and properly trained, those who intend to implement Quality Management should turn to their major responsibility—that of providing quality instruction to the school district's students [23]. The first step in applying QM to students is that of determining outcome-based quality level specifications for the entire group of students' achievement levels (see Figure 8.3). Next,

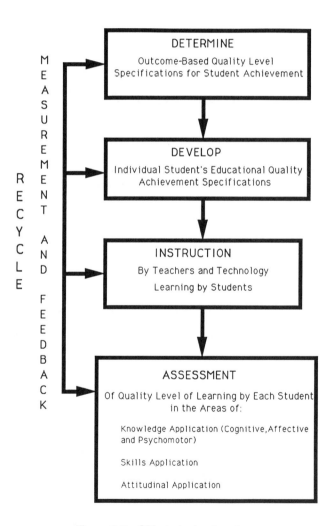

Figure 8.3. QM student subsystem.

each student's quality student achievement specifications must be developed, as students differ in their abilities and past levels of knowledge and achievement. Once the group of students' and each individual student's achievement specifications have been developed, the teachers and admininstrators must determine the most appropriate means of delivering instruction, including the use of technology when it is appropriate to use it in combination with other delivery methodologies. Finally, assessment of the level of quality achievement by each student in the areas of knowledge, skills, and attitudes is completed for the cognitive, affective, and psychomotor areas.

External Environment Subsystem

It is important in any school district that wishes to implement QM to involve external stakeholders (parents, employers, community organizations, citizens) in the process of assisting in determining the quality specifications of the services and products delivered and to involve representatives of various stakeholders groups in assessing the level of success achieved by the school district (see Figure 8.4). Many districts offer adult education, community recreational activities, and community schools programs. In these districts, the services and products offered by the school to the community at large should also be assessed [24].

There are four steps to be included in this process: (1) the QM implementers should develop a needs assessment related to the school district's external environment, and (2) the implementers should arrive at the level of quality services and products delivered by (3) scanning the external environment by use of hard (factual) data (such as employment level of graduates) and soft data (opinions and attitudes related to the services and products provided), by obtaining these data during the formative stages of implementation, and by (4) obtaining summative data to determine the quality of products and services, as perceived by those persons in the external environment during certain predetermined points in time.

Strategic Planning Process Subsystem

The strategic planning process for QM begins with the conduct of a needs assessment of three important groups of individuals: (1) external customers, (2) internal employee customers, and (3) student cus-

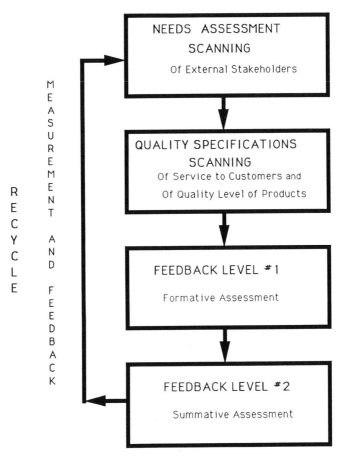

Figure 8.4. QM external environmental subsystem.

tomers. Once a needs assessment is conducted, the soft (opinions or attitudes) and hard (factual) data collected is carefully considered when constructing a school district's vision. In the case of QM, the school district should include customer satisfaction, ever-increasing quality of services and products, two-way communications among all categories of stakeholders, and a collaborative and empowering educational environment as cornerstones of the school district's preferred future vision.

Once the quality vision is agreed upon (see Figure 8.5), strategic goals related to customer satisfaction and quality services and products can be established. Next, the employees are responsible for delivering the quality services and products desired. Finally, the degree to which the deliverables meet the quality specifications are determined by collecting and analyzing data from formative and summative evaluations. Once the data are analyzed, there is a built-in feedback cycle intended to continually improve the quality of each step in the process of developing the services and products to be delivered.

Tactical Planning Process Subsystem

Strategic planning determines the *whats* to be delivered. Once the strategic plans have been determined, tactical (the *hows*) action plans must be laid in order to complete the planning cycle (Figure 8.6).

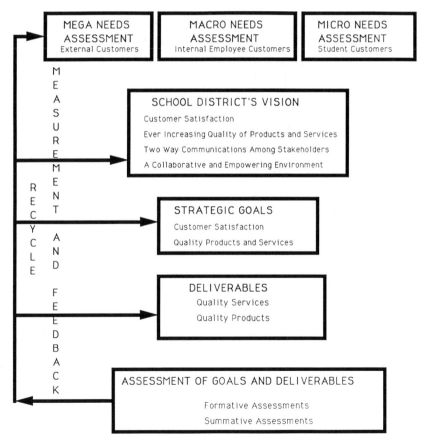

Figure 8.5. QM strategic planning process subsystem.

Again, the tactical planners start with a needs assessment of what currently exists, compared to the what should be (desired future determinations) by the strategic planners. Next, they develop the tactical (how to do it) objectives and the deliverable means for both quality services and quality products. The detailed plans include answers to: (1) why should this action be taken, (2) what activities are to be included, (3) where will the action program be initiated, (4) when will

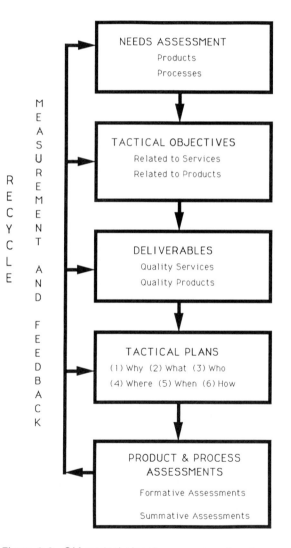

Figure 8.6. QM tactical planning process subsystem.

the action program be initiated, (5) how will the program be initiated, and (6) who will be responsible for seeing that each step of the action plan is implemented at the qualitative level that has been predetermined. Finally, the tactical action plans will be assessed for fidelity by completing formative data collection, feedback, and analyses, and by conducting a summative evaluation of the degree to which the tactical action program has achieved the predetermined qualitative specifications of the products and services delivered.

SUMMARY

This chapter has considered the elements and definitions of Quality Management, defining it as a combination of philosophy, goals, and process. It was described as consisting of the following key concepts:

- It focuses on quality results at each *value-added* step of the development and delivery of each product or service.
- It solicits feedback from both its internal and external customers for the purpose of developing quality specifications for each of its products and services.
- It empowers employees and solicits their ideas to continually improve each product and service.
- It stresses data collection and feedback.
- It relies on planning to achieve a vision of total quality in all aspects of the organization's activities, products, services, and culture.
- Its ultimate challenge is to please each and every customer.

A QM model planning structure was presented with requirements outlined. The management requirements of QM were listed, including the notions of ownership, empowerment, and feedback. The importance of assessing QM programs was stressed, both in a formative and summative fashion, as were its advantages and cautions. These included the need for a mass of stakeholders and the existence of a facilitating culture. The attitudinal, conceptual, and staff development prerequisites for successful QM implementation were described. Following this, the theory-to-practice example was presented, with figures to illustrate an employee subsystem, a student subsystem, an external environment subsystem, a strategic planning process subsystem, and a tactical planning process subsystem.

PRACTICAL EXERCISES

(1) List those individuals and groups *external* to your organization that you consider as your customers. What products(s) and/or services(s) do you deliver to each of these customers?

(2) What methods do you use or could you use to receive feedback from each category of these *external* customers? How do you or how could you use this feedback to improve the quality specifications for your products and/or services?

(3) List those individuals and groups who are *internal* to your organization that you consider as your customers. What product(s) and/or service(s) do you deliver to each of these customers?

(4) What methods do you use or could you use to receive feedback from each category of these *internal* customers? How do you use or how could you use this feedback to improve the quality specifications for your products and/or services?

(5) How would you define *value-added* as this term is applied to your products and/or services? What implications would this *value-added* concept have for the approach you would use to implement and maintain Quality Management in your organization?

(6) What data would you collect to determine the *quality impact* of a value-added approach to Quality Management?

(7) What measures and means would you use to evaluate the effectiveness of your Quality Management program at the (a) formative level and (b) summative level?

REFERENCES

1. Herman, J. J. 1993. "Total Quality Management," *Educational Facilities Planner,* 31(1):30.
2. Bonstingl, J. J. 1993. "The Quality Movement: What's It Really About?" *Educational Leadership,* 51(1):66.
3. Herman, J. J. 1993. *Holistic Quality: Managing, Restructuring, Empowering Schools.* Newbury Park, CA: Corwin Press, Inc., a Sage Publications Company.
4. Johnson, R. S. 1993. "TQM: Leadership for the Quality Transformation, Part 5," *Quality Progress,* 26(5):83–86.
5. Herman, J. J. and J. L. Herman. In press. *Making Change Happen.* Newbury Park, CA: Corwin Press, Inc., a Sage Publications Company.
6. Hill, W. J. 1992. "Value through Quality," *Quality Progress,* 25(5):31–34.

7. Kaufman, R. and J. J. Herman. 1991. *Strategic Planning in Education.* Lancaster, PA: Technomic Publishing Company, Inc., p. 246.

8. Lasher, G. C. 1993. "Quality Schools on a Shoestring," *Thrust for Educational Leadership,* 22(4):8–12.

9. Freeston, K. R. 1992. "Getting Started with TQM," *Educational Leadership,* 50(3):10–13.

10. Herman, J. J. 1992. "Total Quality Management Basics: TQM Comes to School," *School Business Affairs,* 58(4):20–28.

11. Herman, J. J. and J. L. Herman. 1991 *The Positive Development of Human Resources and School District Organizations.* Lancaster, PA: Technomic Publishing Company, Inc., pp. 19–20.

12. Herman, J. J. and J. L. Herman. 1993. *School-Based Management: Current Thinking and Practice.* Springfield, IL: Charles C. Thomas Publisher, pp. 228–230.

13. Herman, J. J. and G. Megiveron. 1993. *Collective Bargaining in Education: Win/Win, Win/Lose, Lose/Lose.* Lancaster, PA: Technomic Publishing Company, Inc.

14. Johnson, R. S. 1993. "TQM: Leadership for the Quality Transformation, Part 3," *Quality Progress,* 26(3):91–94.

15. Scarr, L. E. 1992. "Using Self-Regulating Work Teams," *Educational Leadership,* 50(3):68–70.

16. Bonstingl, J. J. 1992. "The Quality Revolution in Education," *Educational Leadership,* 50(3):4–9.

17. Abernathy, P. E. and R. W. Serfass. 1992. "One District's Improvement Quality Story," *Educational Leadership,* 50(3):14–17.

18. Reiner, C. A. and H. Morris. 1987. "Leadership Development," in *Training and Development Handbook, Third Edition,* Robert L. Craig (ed.), New York, NY: McGraw-Hill, pp. 523–524.

19. Zemke, R. 1993. "A Bluffer's Guide to TQM," *Training,* 30(4):48–55.

20. Hixson, J. and K. Lovelace. 1992. "Total Quality Management's Challenge to Urban Schools," *Educational Leadership,* 50(3):24–27.

21. Herman, J. J. 1993. "Is TQM for Me? A Decision-Making Interrogatory," *School Business Affairs,* 59(4):28–30.

22. Kaufman, R. and A. Hirumi. 1992. "Ten Steps to 'TQM,' " *Educational Leadership,* 50(3):33–34.

23. Dinklocker, C. 1992. "Our Deming Users' Group," *Educational Leadership,* 50(3):32.

24. Isaacson, N. and J. Bamburg. 1992. "Can Schools Become Learning Organizations?" *Educational Leadership,* 50(3):42–44.

CHAPTER 9

Establishing Quality Management
Strategic and Tactical Plans for Schools

THIS chapter discusses (1) strategic and tactical planning definitions; (2) reasons for systematic planning; (3) means of communicating with noncommittee stakeholders; (4) methods of team building and collaborative decision making; (5) detailed steps in planning models; (6) mega, macro, and micro needs assessments and arriving at preferred future vision #1; (7) arriving at consensus about beliefs and values; (8) determining Critical Success Factors (CSF); (9) scanning the external and internal environments; (10) arriving at preferred vision #2; (11) developing a mission statement; (12) developing strategic mega, macro, and micro goals; (13) arriving at decision rules; (14) conducting internal and external S.W.O.T. (strengths, weaknesses, opportunities, and threats) analyses; (16) examples of specific goals; (17) developing action plans that answer why? what? who? when? where? and how?; (18) developing action plans; (19) conducting formative evaluations; (20) doing a summative evaluation; (21) conducting a recycling phase; (22) advantages and cautions related to strategic and tactical planning; (23) key strategic and tactical planning concepts; (24) enabling behaviors and bridges to new practice; and (25) a theory-to-practice example.

Once the local school board members, the superintendent of schools, and other important decision makers decide that formalized planning is to take place continuously within the school district and within the constituent schools, the process of selecting planning partners and planning methodologies must take place. It is important, at this stage, to select planners who think and act strategically and tactically [1].

Probably the best way for the decision makers to act is to create a strategic planning steering committee comprised of a wide variety of stakeholders. These stakeholders should include teachers, principals, parents, community members, business and industrial representatives, central office administrators, students, civic club representatives, and representatives of any other group that is considered influential within the local district. If the steering committee membership appears too large to be an effective group, it is wise to lessen the membership of the steering committee and allow the steering committee to create sub-committees and increase the membership by appointments to these subcommittees.

Once the committee membership has been decided upon and the members are provided with a written charge of duties and responsibilities, an initial set of orientation and training meetings should be conducted [2]. During these training sessions, stress should be placed on (1) defining strategic and tactical planning, (2) spelling out the reasons for the district to do these types of planning, (3) identifying the means of communicating with both committee members and noncommittee stakeholders, (4) outlining the detailed steps of both the strategic and tactical planning processes, and (5) identifying methods of team building and collaborative decision making.

Now that the initial steps in creating a system and structure for continuous planning within the district have been discussed, we can turn to defining the strategic and tactical planning terms.

STRATEGIC AND TACTICAL PLANNING DEFINITIONS

Strategic planning is *long-term* planning to achieve a preferred future *vision.* Without a vision, it is merely long-term planning that may or may not improve the schools. It is sad, but true, that many times we are doing a tremendous job of unimportant things while not focusing on those things that are crucial to the success of schools. It is also true that without a vision of *what should be,* we could arrive (like the driver who wanted to go to Chicago but ended up in San Francisco because he didn't plan to arrive at his desired destination) at mediocrity as an end result. Strategic planning deals with the *whats,* while tactical planning deals with the *hows* [3].

In contrast to strategic planning, *tactical planning* focuses on the specific means designed to ultimately receive the *whats* (strategic goals). This is the planning that deals with the details of operation. In all probability, it is wise, at this point, to eliminate the nonemployee stakeholders from the planning activities. Of course, some nonemployees may be included if they have specific expertise to lend to the tasks involved [4].

However, once the nonemployee stakeholders complete their strategic planning activities and provide the strategic goals to the tactical planners, the nonemployees must still be presented with periodic progress updates on both the tactical plans and the results achieved on the strategic goals.

REASONS FOR SYSTEMATIC PLANNING

If one does not know the destination to be attained, then one will end in a detouring state *ad infinitum*. For a school district to improve, there must be a vision of what the district should look like at some point in the future, and then a structure and processes should be put in place to cause that vision to be achieved. The local functionaries should clearly explain to all of its stakeholders the various reasons for doing systematic planning. Some of the main reasons should include the following [5,6]:

- A sincere desire must be present to involve a wide variety of stakeholders in the school district's decision making and planning in order to acquire broad-based support for and ownership of the school district's services, products, and programs.
- Committee membership of representative stakeholders can generate a critical mass of support from the community at large, the district's employees, and the district's students. This can be accomplished by selling the vision and the benefits of the planning activities to all stakeholders.
- Collectively, it should be stressed that they must determine the preferred future vision of what they desire the school district to look like at some future point in time. This must include the specific results that are expected in both the services and products provided by the school district.
- Once the committee has agreed upon the results to be achieved and that will indicate when the preferred future vision has been reached, the committee members can compare those desired results with the results currently being achieved. This comparison of what is to what should be will identify the needs to be met.
- Finally, once the needs are so identified, the tactical planners can then develop specific action plans that are designed to achieve the desired results that will lead to achievement of the specific objectives, the strategic goals, and, ultimately, the preferred future vision that is desired.

MEANS OF COMMUNICATING WITH
NONCOMMITTEE STAKEHOLDERS

While the members of the strategic and tactical planning committees go about their work, they must not forget the importance of clear and continuing two-way communication with all of the stakeholders of the school district. No matter how broadly representative of the stakeholders the committee is, and no matter how many stakeholders are serving on the planning subcommittees, they comprise a very insignificant mass of the total stakeholders that are located in the school district. Therefore, some methods of keeping the communication open and continuing must be utilized. Some of the more helpful means of doing this include (1) announcing all planning meetings in advance and allowing all meetings to be open to any stakeholder, (2) sending periodic written reports of activities and results, (3) providing speakers to various groups within the community, and (4) providing information on the specific plans and allowing for input from all stakeholders before finalizing and initiating those plans [7].

METHODS OF TEAM BUILDING AND COLLABORATIVE
DECISION MAKING

For the strategic and tactical planning committee stakeholder members who have probably not worked together before and who may not have been previously involved in collaborative planning efforts, it is crucial that they are given training in some areas even prior to starting their detailed planning tasks. It will save time and avoid conflict if this training precedes the actual work sessions. Such matters as communication skills, conflict resolution skills, and activities that build trust and respect should be included.

DETAILED STEPS IN PLANNING MODELS

Once the stakeholders understand what strategic and tactical planning is all about; once they understand the reasons for doing this systematic planning; once they understand the requirement of communicating with stakeholders at large to build a critical mass of support and ownership; and once they are provided with some skill training in the areas of communications, team building, and collaborative decision making, they can be introduced to the detailed steps in both the strategic and tactical planning processes [9].

Two models will present a visual view of the details that are discussed. Figure 9.1 presents the steps involved in strategic planning. The shaded area, objectives for goals, represents the point at which the strategic planners turn over their work to the tactical planners, and it is the point at which the nonemployee stakeholders are probably thanked and relieved of their assignment. This objectives step is one that may be completed by the strategic planners, or it may be delegated to the tactical planners. Figure 9.2 presents the detailed steps that must be accomplished by the tactical planners.

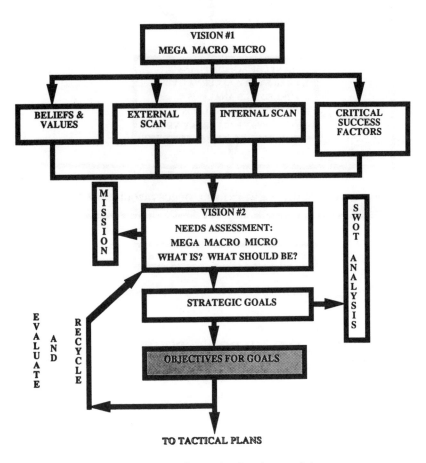

Figure 9.1. Strategic planning model.

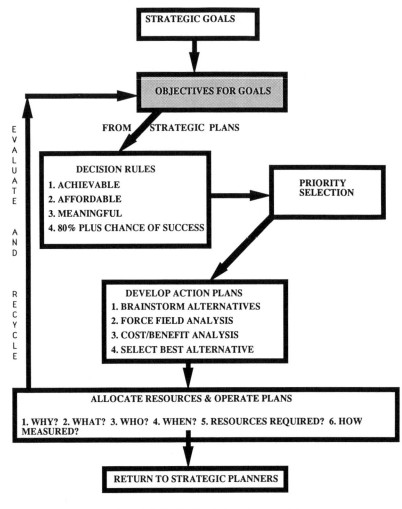

Figure 9.2. Tactical planning model.

MEGA, MACRO, AND MICRO NEEDS ASSESSMENTS AND PREFERRED VISION #1

The strategic planning model illustrated in Figure 9.1 indicates that there are two visioning steps. This is suggested because the stakeholders should initially be allowed to dream about what they want the school district and all its components to look like at some point five, ten, or more years into the future. This is the initial step where the stakeholders identify their preferred future vision. Once they do this, without the constraints of specific information gathering to discourage them or to retard the initial progress, the stakeholders have to collect data; and, then, based upon this information, they determine a final vision of what the preferred future should or could become. In both visioning exercises, the strategic planning committee should identify the mega (societal) needs that the school district and its component parts must address, the macro (total organizational) needs that must be addressed, and the micro (subcomponent) needs that must be addressed [10].

Once the initial preferred future vision is agreed upon by the strategic planning stakeholder committee members, the committee must collect data to determine if modifications are to be made in their initial vision. Of course, the strategic planning committee may wish to appoint subcommittees to assist in this data-gathering phase of strategic planning.

ARRIVING AT CONSENSUS ABOUT BELIEFS AND VALUES

Before vision #2 is agreed to, it is important that the members of the stakeholders' strategic planning committee agree on the core beliefs and values that will guide further planning. This statement, once consensus has been reached, should be placed in writing and widely distributed. It should deal with the core beliefs held by the committee members regarding students, teachers, administrators, other employees, parents, and the community at large [11]. It also should address the instructional programs, instructional delivery systems, and instructional monitoring systems of results. Merely by illustrating a few plausible beliefs and values, it will assist in demonstrating the types of statements that should be placed into a written format and widely distributed [12].

- All students can learn.
- Students and their learning are the primary purposes of schools and the instructional programs. Therefore, these purposes should be used as a decision screen for any decisions made in this school district. Decisions that support these purposes or that supplement these purposes should be implemented; decisions that are contrary to these purposes should not be implemented.

- Collaborative decision making with representatives of all stakeholders is favored.
- Research in such areas as cooperative learning should be carefully studied and, if proven effective, should become a choice instructional delivery alternative.
- Strategic and tactical planning should become an integral part of the management functions of the school district and the individual schools. More importantly, strategic and tactical thinking should be emphasized and rewarded and should become part of the organization's culture.
- Students, parents, employees, and citizens should be considered valued customers; and they should be treated with the respect and courtesy that each employee would desire for herself/himself.

DETERMINING CRITICAL SUCCESS FACTORS

Another activity that should be conducted by the strategic planners, prior to reaching consensus on vision #2, is that of identifying the Critical Success Factors (CSFs) [13]. In every organization, only a very few items can be truly critical to success. If these are identified and used as focus points for planning, this procedure can eliminate much administrivia, paperwork, and unnecessary communication.

In practically all school districts or school buildings, the CSFs should probably number no more than eight. Four CSFs will illustrate this point:

- Student achievement at, or above, the predicted level is critical; and this should be carefully and continuously monitored.
- Teachers and administrators who truly believe that *all* students can learn are critical, and observation of their actions should provide witness that they are operating within this belief.
- Treating students, parents, and community members as the individual employee wishes to be treated is critical.
- Open and collaborative planning and communications with all stakeholders is critical.

SCANNING THE EXTERNAL AND INTERNAL ENVIRONMENTS

The scanning of data to locate trends that may impact the preferred future vision, strategic goals, and/or tactical plans must be conducted prior to arriving at vision #2, as these data are crucial elements that make planning both efficient and effective. Not only should the scanning be both external to the school and/or school district, but it also should be internal. The data should be collected for a number of years to indicate the trends that may impact planning. These trends will allow the planners to decide what is possible to accomplish, what specific actions to initiate which will take advantage of positive trends, and, also, what actions to initiate to lessen or overcome negative trends. Many times, these trends will also provide information for the establishment of needs; and they certainly must be seriously considered prior to the stakeholders' strategic planning committee arriving at consensus on vision #2. A few internal and external hypothetical scanning trends will illustrate this point [14].

Identified *internal trends* indicate that an increasingly higher percentage of crack children are entering the schools, and the district has an in-migration of refugees from countries and races that were not previously present. Identified *external trends* indicate that numerous private schools are beginning to appear in the district and the student dropout rate has increased by 22% over the past ten years. Once the stakeholders' strategic planning committee has (1) arrived at a consensus statement of core beliefs and values, (2) agreed upon the CSFs, and (3) completed internal and external scans of data to determine long-term trends that may impact the district's and schools' strategic and tactical planning, the strategic planning committee can arrive at its preferred future vision #2. This vision will include mega (societal), macro (total district), and micro (individual building and other subsets) indicators. The what should be or what could be scenario, in essence, becomes the agreed-upon preferred future vision [15].

Once the what should be or what could be state desired in the future is agreed upon, the strategic planning committee can determine the needs (gaps between what is and what should be or what could be) to be met. Once the needs are identified, the committee can develop a written mission statement and develop a list of strategic goals intended to meet the identified needs.

ARRIVING AT PREFERRED VISION #2

Now that the stratetic planning committee has in hand its description of its vision #1, has collected data and determined potential influential trends by scanning, decided upon its beliefs and values, and determined the CSFs, it is ready to determine its vision #2. This is a very important step that will take a great deal of time to develop because this vision will determine the parameters for all future planning efforts.

DEVELOPING A MISSION STATEMENT

In general, a mission statement should be a tightly written, rather short, and easily understood statement of the primary focus of the school district or the individual school. A high school's mission may be different from an elementary school's vision, and a special education department's vision may differ from that of a magnet school. If this statement can be written in a single sentence, this will be helpful. If necessary, this single sentence mission can be elaborated upon by indicating how the school or district intends to implement the mission. In any case, even after the implementation statements are added, the mission statement and elaboration should *never* reach more than a single page in length.

DEVELOPING STRATEGIC MEGA, MACRO, AND MICRO GOALS

Once the vision and mission activities have been completed, the strategic planners must identify the goals that are to be achieved in the future. This is a very important step in the strategic planning process, for it is the beginning of providing the detailed directions and foci road maps for the tactical planners and for those who will be held responsible for managing the operations intended to achieve the desired results [16]. Strategic goals are broad directional statements that are designed to guide those persons who are to devise and manage programs and activities to achieve the stated goals. A few examples will illustrate this point:

- The achievement level in the core subjects of reading, math, and science will be improved, when compared to past achievement patterns, by those students who are identified as being at risk.
- The dropout rate for high school students will be reduced.
- Vandalism in all school buildings will be reduced.

It is also important that the strategic planning committee consider three types of goals—mega (societal), macro (total organization), and micro (subsets of the organization)—because the schools and school districts must also be partially responsible for assisting in some areas of needs (gaps between what is and what should be) in society. An example of a goal related to a mega need is that all students shall be required to perform some service to the community prior to graduation from high school.

ARRIVING AT DECISION RULES

Because there may be a great number of goals arrived at by the strategic planning committee, there must be some method of arriving at goal priorities. This is important, not only for prioritizing strategic goals, but the same rules can be used to later determine priorities among numerous specific tactical objectives and among various potential action plans.

The committee should arrive at some commonsense rules similar to the following [17]:

- Is it doable?
- Is it affordable?
- Is there an 80% or greater chance of success?

The 80% or greater chance of success can vary with time. If a committee is new, it is important that they initially have success. If they do not, the members will feel that they put in a great deal of effort only to fail. In such a situation, morale will suffer, a defeatist attitude may well develop, the effort of the member will diminish, and many members may resign. However, if the goals selected are successful, the members will feel great about their efforts; and they will be ready to tackle more difficult goals.

With a seasoned committee that has been strength bombarded for some time period, the percent of success on a very important goal may be as low as 10%. At this point, the experienced committee members can deal with partial success as well as total success.

CONDUCTING INTERNAL AND EXTERNAL
S.W.O.T. ANALYSES

Once the strategic goals have been identified and agreed to by the stakeholders' strategic planning committee, an S.W.O.T. (strengths, weaknesses, opportunities, and threats) analysis should be conducted of both the internal and external environments within which the individual school or the school district exists. The purpose of this step is to determine: (1) which factors or variables are identified as strengths and to plan on capitalizing upon them in a manner that will assist in achieving the strategic goals, (2) which factors or variables are identified as weaknesses and to develop improvement plans to overcome them, (3) which factors or variables are identified as untapped opportunities that can be capitalized upon, and (4) which factors or variables are threats to the achievement of the strategic goals and to plan means of eliminating or lessening their negative impacts [18].

A few examples of both internal and external factors or variables will illustrate this matter:

(1) External factors or variables
  • The scanning trendline indicates that the school district's tax base is decreasing (external threat).
  • Demographic scanning trendlines indicate that numerous retired citizens have recently moved into the school district, and this provides an opportunity to increase the number of school volunteers (external opportunity).
  • The district, not the individual schools, has involved external stakeholders in its planning activities (external weakness).
  • A parental attitude survey indicates a high degree of satisfaction with the education their children are receiving (external strength).

(2) Internal factors or variables
  • The student dropout rate is very low, and it is decreasing (internal strength).
  • There is an extremely large teacher turnover rate (internal weakness).
  • Advanced placement courses have very low student enrollments; and, if this continues, the courses will have to be eliminated for financial (cost/benefit) reasons (internal threat).
  • Cooperative learning, if implemented, will provide a delivery system that has proven successful in improving both the school climate and the achievement levels of many students (internal opportunity).

Once the internal and external S.W.O.T. analysis has been completed, there may be some cases where the original strategic goals must be modified; but, generally, the process can be moved next to the step of determining the specific objectives that are intended to identify more clearly the detailed desired results to be subsumed beneath each strategic goal statement [19]. This step may be performed by the stakeholders' strategic planning committee, or the committee may wish to merely present the strategic goals and request that the tactical planners develop the specific objectives for each goal. Whichever group deals with the specific goals, there is a recycling requirement to ensure that the specific objectives and the strategic goals are aligned and synchronized and that the strategic planning and the tactical planning phases are closely articulated. In this case, it is assumed that the strategic planners have requested that the tactical planners develop the specific objectives.

SPECIFIC OBJECTIVES

Before moving on to the action planning stage of tactical planning, a couple of examples will illustrate some specific objectives that might be subsumed under strategic goals.

Example one, related to the strategic goal of decreasing the percentage of high school student dropouts, might well read: within five years, the percentage of high school student dropouts will decrease by 40% when compared to the dropout numbers for the current year.

Example two, related to the goal of involving more internal and external stakeholders in the decisions made at the individual school buildings, might well be stated as: within one year, each school building in the school district shall have initiated a school-based management committee comprised of the principal, students, parents, teachers, and community members; and within three years, at least 90% of the participants will have indicated that they perceive that their local school's services and products have improved because of the stakeholders' involvement in decision making at the local school building level.

DEVELOPING ACTION PLANS

Action planning includes the following activities: (1) establishing priorities among the various objectives by utilizing an agreed-upon set of decision rules; (2) developing tactical planning alternates by performing the techniques of (a) brainstorming, (b) force-field analyses, and (c) sometimes conducting a cost/benefit analysis; (3) selecting the best *fit* alternative action plan that appears to have the greatest probability of achieving the specific objective; and (4) determining answers to the who? what? when? why? where? and how measured? questions. Briefly, each step is reviewed below:

- Developing a set of priority-establishing decision rules involves agreeing upon some commonsense rules to be used if there are too many objectives to be dealt with at any point in time. Those that are the most important should be dealt with initially, while the others are placed in a later time sequence. Commonsense decision rules might well include: (1) the objectives appear to be clearly achievable, (2) they can be achieved in an affordable manner, (3) they are truly meaningful, and (4) they have an 80% or better chance of success. This standard of 80% in the initial stages is important to allow the planners, early on, to enjoy success for their efforts. Later on, however, this standard can be lowered considerably as the planners have built sufficient self-confidence to attack truly difficult assignments.

- Conducting brainstorming activities follows the determination of the priority goals to be addressed. Once the goals are established, it is important to brainstorm possible means or tactics to achieve them. The initial step in arriving at a variety of alternative action program solutions can best be completed by brainstorming ideas. If the brainstorming is conducted in accordance with rigorous rules, it can generate as many as 100 ideas in a very short period of time. The key to making this initial step in arriving at potential solutions is to allow all participants to present ideas as quickly as possible and to do this without concern about the initial practicality of the ideas, for sometimes the wildest-appearing initial ideas become the best alternatives. The rules of brainstorming are: (1) all ideas are acceptable, (2) creativity is encouraged, (3) there is no discussion when the idea is presented in this format, (4) the suggester is not to elaborate or explain the idea, and (5) participants do not, verbally or nonverbally, indicate approval or disapproval of any idea. Once the initial brainstorming session ends (usually lasting less than fifteen minutes when the rules are used), it is time to discuss each suggestion and determine those that seem to offer the most promise. At this time, there may be additional information sought out on some of the initial suggestions before the list of possibilities is completely narrowed.

- Doing a force-field analysis is an excellent next step, once the list of possible action programs has been narrowed to those that seem to offer the best possibilities. This step involves listing all the supportive and constraining indicators for each of the alternative action programs.
- Performing a cost/benefit analysis is sometimes required. This procedure involves computing the cost of the action program suggested and comparing the cost to the anticipated benefits to be received. If the predicted benefits exceed the cost, the program should be implemented. Conversely, if the predicted benefits are less than the cost, the program should be eliminated from further consideration.
- Selecting the best fit alternative becomes a rather simple matter with the above information at hand.
- Addressing the interrogatories follows the selection of the best alternative proposed action program to achieve the specific objective addressed. At this stage, a simple chart should be made to indicate the following. (1) Why is this program being attempted? (2) What are the detailed tasks to be completed to implement this action program? (3) Who is to be responsible for achieving each task? (4) When is each task to be completed? (5) Where will the program be offered? (6) How is each task to be completed? (7) What resources are required to complete each task? (8) How will the degree of achievement of the task be measured and judged?

CONDUCTING FORMATIVE EVALUATIONS

Before the action plan is implemented, a method of evaluating the degree of impact and success *during the operation* of the plan should be developed. It is unwise to wait until the entire plan's activities have been completed before determining the impact and degree of success achieved by the action plan. This *formative evaluation* structure should become an integral part of the action planning stage for each action plan that is developed and made operational.

DOING A SUMMATIVE EVALUATION

Simply evaluating action plans while they are in process and making logical adjustments if such adjustments are needed are insufficient for a total evaluation structure. Although formative evaluations can lead to in-process corrections, an end-of-process evaluation is also required. These *summative evaluations* will determine the final degree of success the individual and collective action plans have attained when compared to the original specific objectives and the controlling strategic goal.

CONDUCTING A RECYCLING PHASE

It is important to include a recycling phase into the tactical planning scheme, as resultant information should lead to continuous improvements. If modifications of specific objectives are required or if entirely new action plans have to be developed, a built-in recycling phase will make this a mandatory activity.

ADVANTAGES AND CAUTIONS RELATED TO STRATEGIC AND TACTICAL PLANNING

There are many advantages and a few cautions that must be mentioned to those individuals and groups who are empowered to carry out strategic and tactical planning activities in school districts or in individual school buildings; some of the main ones require identification.

Advantages

- They cause decisions makers to think about long-term, desired results before taking actions.
- They cause decision makers to develop specific measurable objectives and to collect data to determine if the desired results were met to the qualitative and quantitative degree originally specified. They also cause the decision makers to complete the programs within the timelines and within the resources allocated.
- They cause people to *think* strategically and tactically.
- They cause involvement of internal and external stakeholders in the planning activities and, thereby, build in broad-based ownership of the planning process and the desired results.

- Most importantly, they cause planners to (1) spell out a desired preferred future vision for the school district and/or school building, (2) determine what the current state looks like, (3) identify specific needs (gaps between the desired future state and the existing state), and (4) develop action programs to eliminate the gaps.

Cautions

- In a school setting, this will not be successful unless a wide variety of stakeholders are involved in the planning, and they buy into the purposes, goals, and action programs.
- These planning activities will be doomed to failure if they are used as a quick fix, as this is a long-term and continuing commitment.
- These activities will not be successful if: (1) beliefs and values are not agreed upon; (2) a clear vision of the preferred future is not determined; (3) scanning is not done; (4) action programs, based on strategic goals and specific objectives, are not developed; and (5) monitoring, valuating, and recycling activities are not built into the planning process.

KEY STRATEGIC AND TACTICAL PLANNING CONCEPTS

The key strategic and tactical planning concepts are: (1) stakeholders must be empowered to be a part of the planning and decision-making bodies; (2) desired future results, which, when combined, identify a preferred future vision, are crucial to success; (3) action programs must be developed, which will lead to successfull achievement of the specific objectives, the strategic goals, and the preferred future vision; and (4) monitoring, feedback, evaluation, and recycling activities must be used to determine if the needs (gaps between what should be or what could be and what is) have been met and the preferred future vision achieved.

ENABLING BEHAVIORS AND BRIDGES TO NEW PRACTICE

The training implied by the implementation of viable strategic and tactical planning is substantive; undertaking the process itself is a training experience, one best handled by individuals versed in such training. In view of the need for the active and undistracted participation of all school district members in the planning process, it is desirable that such training be conducted by trainers and facilitators from outside the school district, rather than by a member of the administrative team. It is also helpful, when dealing with the external stakeholder activities, to build on existing parent and community relationships as bridges to more meaningful participation and to ensure the requisite wide variety. Given the long-term commitment of effective strategic and tactical planning, some pre-awareness and attitudinal-oriented staff development, which emphasizes the demands of systematic change, would be helpful in creating a hospitable climate for such planning. Both this and skills in collaboration and shared decision making should be built in advance of attempting planning training and implementation [20,21].

THEORY-TO-PRACTICE EXAMPLE

As a means of briefly illustrating the entire strategic and tactical planning processes, the hypothetical Great School District will serve as an example. The strategic planning committee of Great School District has arrived at the following agreements after many days of planning.

STRATEGIC PLANNERS' AGREEMENTS

A *vision* has been developed that includes the following: (1) all students will be cognizant of the requirement to be of service to their community (mega level); (2) all employees will be competent, efficient, and effective (macro level); and (3) each individual school within the district shall possess a school climate that includes a caring attitude, a safe and healthy environment, and a focused high aspirational level for each student's academic and social achievement.

Beliefs were agreed upon that include the following: (1) all students can learn what is taught, and (2) a wide variety of stakeholders have to be involved in important decision making at both the individual school and the school district levels.

Internal and external scanning activities discovered trends that included: (1) an increasing student dropout rate, (2) decreasing levels of student achievement in the areas of science and mathematics, (3) an increase of retired persons living in the school district, (4) a decrease in the percentage of financial support provided by the state and the federal government, (5) a positive attitude toward the schools by 85% of the school district's residents.

Critical Success Factors were determined to include: (1) high achievement levels by students; (2) general individual citizens' and businesses' and other governmental groups' support; and (3) a productive, efficient, and effective group of teachers, classified employees, and administrators.

A *S.W.O.T.* (strengths, weaknesses, opportunities, and threats) analysis discovered that: (1) the population trend was that of an aging group percentage (both threat and opportunity); (2) local taxpayers' attitudes are becoming more favorable toward the schools (strength); (3) the local teachers' union has become more and more negative toward the board of education and the school district's administrators (threat); and (4) reading test scores of elementary students are well below norm (weakness).

Specific measurable objectives that were developed included: (1) the percentage of high school student dropouts will be reduced by 50% over the current dropout pattern within an eight-year period, and (2) elementary reading test scores, on a national norm-referenced test, will display a 20% improvement within the next four years.

Although this specific measurable objectives step may be completed by the strategic planners, the strategic planners may chose to provide the tactical planners with the opportunity to develop the specific measurable objectives that fall beneath each of the strategic goals that have been developed by the strategic planners.

A *recycling* plan has been put into place in case future changes develop in external and/or internal trendline data, Critical Success Factors, beliefs and values, or data from S.W.O.T. analyses demonstrate existence of changes that are significant enough to cause the strategic planners to modify their vision, mission, or strategic goals.

TACTICAL PLANNERS' DECISIONS

Decision rules were identified to allow the prioritization of the strategic goals, specific objectives, and/or action plans. The three rules agreed upon included: is it affordable; is it predictable, effective, and efficient; and is it meaningful?

Brainstorming was used by the tactical planners to arrive at eighty-five potential alternative plans to solve the requirement to improve students' reading test scores. Formal brainstorming rules were used, and they included: (1) all suggestions are valid; (2) there is no discussion of the item or questions asked or answered during the brainstorming exercise; (3) there is no criticism or support or any suggestion during this exercise; and (4) creativity of suggestions is promoted.

A force field analysis was completed next for each brainstorming suggestion that was determined to be feasible. This analysis developed a listing of supportive and restraining factors for each action program that was to be considered.

A cost/benefit analysis was next completed for those action programs that survived after consideration of the data from the force field analysis. This analysis assisted the tactical planners in determining which action plans would produce a benefit equal to or exceeding the cost of each action plan. The *best alternative* action program designed to achieve each objective was selected next for implementation.

Resource allocations were determined next. These resources include financial, human, materials and supplies, and temporal resources.

Formative evaluations were carried on during the operation of the action plans, and modifications and corrections were made when it was evident that adjustments were required.

Results data were provided to the strategic planners, and *recycling activities* were begun. This final activity assures coordination between the tactical and strategic planning processes and planners, and it ensures a continuation of both strategic and tactical activities.

Celebrations of all successes took place. *It is imperative that all involved take time to celebrate and publicize each success, admit each failure, and inform all that the planners will try again to continuously reach for the preferred future vision.*

SUMMARY

This chapter has discussed the basic elements and dynamic components of strategic and tactical planning. The creation of planning committees was described as a starting point for the initiation of this implementation. Definitions were provided for both types of planning, focusing on the long-term, vision-infused nature of strategic planning. The reasons for systematic planning were listed, including the desire to plan with broad stakeholder representation, with the intention of arriving at a planned future point. The frequent and comprehensive means of communicating with noncommittee stakeholders and methods of team building and collaborative decision making were described. Such methods should be built in, in advance of attempting training. The detailed steps in planning were illustrated with strategic and tactical models. The conducting of mega, macro, and micro needs assessments and arriving at preferred future vision #1 were outlined, emphasizing the collective process and output dimensions. The steps required to arrive at consensus about beliefs and valueswere described, illustrated with a list of sample beliefs and values. The identification of the CSFs and the scanning of the external and internal environments were presented as two planning steps, requiring a limited and concentrated focus, and the informed and comprehensive consideration of the impact of inside and outside forces. These preceding steps were presented as prerequisites to arriving at a second preferred vision.

The development of a succinct and district primary-focus mission statement precedes the development of strategic mega, macro, and micro goals—the broad directional statements, at the three levels of school, district, and society, which will guide the subsequent operational/tactical planning. The determination of practical decision rules was described as aimed at prioritization, and the conducting of an internal and external S.W.O.T. (strengths, weaknesses, opportunities, and threats) analysis was presented as a step aimed at determining the strengths and needs that may modify identified goals and objectives. The development of action plans to carry out the goals and objectives was described as utilizing a number of activities that will generate tactical planning alternates. The conducting of formative and summative evaluations should be established to assess the in-progress effectiveness of the planning process, and a recycling phase should be built in to ensure continuous improvement. A description of the planning process's advantages and cautions preceded a list of key strategic and tactical planning concepts. The training and climate/culture prerequisites of this planning model were included, prior to the presentation of a theory-to-practice example, which traced the strategic and tactical planning process steps through the vehicle of a hypothetical school district.

PRACTICAL EXERCISES

(1) Determine the internal and external trends that exist in your school district, and assess the potential impact of each.

(2) Decide upon the stakeholders that you would feel it advisable to include in the formation of a districtwide planning committee.

(3) Considering the likely needs of your district, what action programs would be required to meet those identified areas?

(4) Design your personal vision for the district five or more years in the future.

(5) Determine the Critical Success Factors for your district.

(6) Identify the elements and structures, such as built-in assessment processes, which already exist within your district, and which could be converted or employed as components of a strategic and tactical planning process.

REFERENCES

1. Herman, J. J. and J. L. Herman. In press. *Making Change Happen.* Newbury Park, CA: Corwin Press, Inc., a Sage Publications Company.

2. Herman, J. J. and J. L. Herman. 1991. *The Positive Development of Human Resources and School District Organizations.* Lancaster, PA: Technomic Publishing Company, Inc., pp. 19–20.

3. Herman, J. J. 1993. *Holistic Quality: Managing, Restructuring, Empowering Schools.* Newbury Park, CA: Corwin Press, Inc., a Sage Publications Company.

4. Kaufman, R., J. J. Herman and K. Watters. Forthcoming. *Planning Educational Systems: What, When, How.* Lancaster, PA: Technomic Publishing Co., Inc.

5. Kaufman, R. and J. J. Herman. 1991. *Strategic Planning in Education.* Lancaster, PA: Technomic Publishing Company, Inc., p. 246.

6. Kaufman, R. and J. J. Herman. 1991. "Strategic Planning for a Better Society," *Educational Leadership,* 48(7):4–8.

7. Herman, J. J. 1989. "A Vision for the Future: Site-Based Strategic Planning," *NASSP Bulletin,* 73(518):23–27.

8. Jablonski, J. R. 1992. *Implementing TQM: Competing in the Nineties through Total Quality Management, Second Edition.* San Diego, CA: Pfeiffer & Company, pp. 67–72.

9. Killion, J. P. and B. Kaylor. 1991. "Follow-Up: The Key to Training for Transfer," *Journal of Staff Development,* 12(1):64–67.

10. Herman, J. J. and R. Kaufman. 1991. "Making the Mega Plan," *The American School Board Journal,* 178(5):24–25, 41.

11. Kaufman, R. and J. J. Herman. 1989. "Planning That Fits Every District: Three Choices Help Define Your Plan's Scope," *The School Administrator,* 46(8):17–19.

12. Herman, J. J. 1989. "A Vision for the Future: Site-Based Strategic Planning," *NASSP Bulletin,* 73(518):23–27.
13. Kaufman and Herman, 1991. "Strategic Planning for a Better Society," pp. 4–8.
14. Herman, J. J. and J. L. Herman. 1993. *School-Based Management: Current Thinking and Practice.* Springfield, IL: Charles C. Thomas, Publisher, pp. 228–230.
15. Herman and Herman. In press.
16. Herman, J. J. and G. Megiveron. 1993. *Collective Bargaining in Education: Win/Win, Win/Lose, Lose/Lose.* Lancaster, PA: Technomic Publishng Company, Inc.
17. Herman, J. J. 1990. "Action Plans to Make Your Vision a Reality," *NASSP Bulletin,* 74(523):14–17.
18. Herman, J. J. 1989. "External and Internal Scanning: Identifying Variables That Affect Your School," *NASSP Bulletin,* 73(520):48–52.
19. Herman, J. J. 1989. "Strategic Planning—One of the Changing Leadership Roles of the Principal," *The Clearing House,* 63(2):56–58.
20. Kinlaw, D. C. 1992. *Continuous Improvement and Measurement for Total Quality.* San Diego, CA: Pfeiffer & Company, p. 82.
21. Caroselli, M. 1992. *Quality-Driven Designs.* San Diego, CA: Pfeiffer and Company, pp. 67–72.

CHAPTER 10

Combining TQM, Strategic/Tactical Planning, Effective Schools, School-Based and Outcome-Based Management into a Holistic EQM Change Model

THIS chapter discusses (1) Educational Quality Management (EQM) as an integrating catalyst for change; (2) a strategic planning model and a tactical planning model as vehicles for change; (3) Total Quality Management (TQM) as the ultimate quest to be attained; (4) Effective Schools Correlates as guidepoints for the development of strategic goals; (5) School-Based Management (SBM) as an empowerment structure; (6) Outcome-Based Education (OBE) as a measurement technique; (7) model of a powerful, systematic, and integrated operating system for schools; (8) design of a holistic approach to Educational Quality Management; (9) a theory-to-practice example; and (10) enabling behaviors and bridges to new practice.

EDUCATIONAL QUALITY MANAGEMENT: AN INTEGRATING CATALYST FOR CHANGE

No matter what approach a school district utilizes to improve its schools, change is involved. All of the currently favored programs that hold promise for improving our schools (Quality Management, School-Based Management, Effective Schools, strategic and tactical planning, and Outcome-Based Education) involve changes in the traditional ways schools and school districts operate. Whether that change becomes truly systematic transformational change, ending in improved results and a more positive organizational culture, or whether it becomes only a cosmetic and short-term attempt that results in visibility with no results depends on many variables [1,2]. The most important of these variables include

- ownership by a critical mass of stakeholders
- a preferred future vision
- goals and specific objectives

- results orientation
- action-oriented planning
- monitoring and feedback
- evaluation and recycling
- adequate temporal, financial, and human resources

Systematic change, to be successfully implemented, must have a dual focus on the organizational aspects of the organization; and both of these foci must be dealt with simultaneously. First, the restructuring must focus on the development and the interrelationships of all the main components of the system—for any organization, such as a school district, must be thought of in a holistic manner that includes its subunits such as the individual school building. Second, the restructuring must simultaneously focus on the (1) structural components, (2) process components, and (3) cultural components of the total organization and each of its subunits.

If school districts or individual schools are to be transformationally and systematically changed so that the culture is redefined in a manner that promotes dramatic positive changes in the structures, processes, and attitudes that have traditionally existed, the school district or individual school has a much greater probability of success if it unifies and articulates the various promising change programs into a coordinated single approach to its newly designed systematic and restructured organizational culture [3]. The purpose of the remaining discussions is to present and promote proposals for the use of the school district's stakeholders who wish to utilize the discrete school improvement and restructuring programs currrently being promoted in a unified, coordinated, and holistic manner to achieve improvement of their school district's and school building's products and services [4].

STRATEGIC AND TACTICAL PLANNING MODELS: VEHICLES FOR CHANGE

Any holistic approach that intends to combine various change programs into an articulated single approach must first determine the planning structure that will be the primary vehicle around which the other change programs will be gathered. It seems only reasonable that the strategic and tactical planning models be utilized as the primary vehicle for systematic and restructured change. The strategic and tactical planning models to be used for this purpose are presented in Figures 10.1 and 10.2.

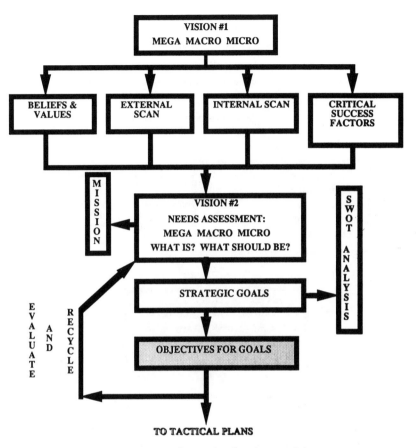

Figure 10.1. Strategic planning model.

Strategic planning deals with the *whats* results to be achieved and tactical planning deals with the *hows* to accomplish the results that are desired. Before elaborating on the steps involved in strategic planning that lead to defining the whats and prior to elaborating upon the tactical planning steps that lead to the hows, it is important to emphasize four points that are inherent in the models: (1) both models assume involvement of representative stakeholders who believe in the planning processes and who will be intricately involved in the planning activities; (2) planning is continuous, and the strategic planners deliver their what statements to the tactical planners who develop the hows. Once the hows have been developed, implemented, and evaluated, the tactical planners return their findings to the strategic planners who begin the next cycle; (3) both models have an evaluation and recycling process included; and (4) the objectives step, indicated as a shaded area in both

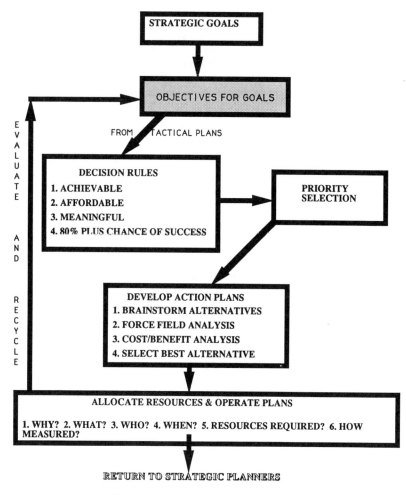

Figure 10.2. Tactical planning model.

figures, implies that this step may be conducted by the strategic planners or that the strategic planners may wish to delegate this responsibility to the tactical planners [5].

Now, let's turn to a brief explanation of all the steps involved in both the strategic and tactical planning models.

Strategic Planning Model's Steps

Step one: In this step, the stakeholders involved in strategic planning define their vision of what should be or what could be at some distant point (five or more years) in the future, and they detail what their organization or school district will look like at that future point. This step could be titled the unsubstantiated preferred future vision because it is done before data are collected to determine what exists today and what trends appear during the data analysis. This vision, as does vision #2, includes mega (societal), macro (total school district), and micro (individual schools and other subunits) components to the overall preferred future vision for the school district [6].

This unsubstantiated, or wish condition, approach is suggested because a newly organized strategic planning committee may lose interest if the members must collect and analyze mounds of data *before* they become action oriented. This also later provides a comparative quality check when vision #2 is developed.

Step two A: This step can start with any of the four activities listed: (1) beliefs and values, (2) external scan, (3) internal scan, or (4) Critical Success Factors (CSF); or all four may be tackled simultaneously. The important point is that all four information sources should be completed *before* the strategic stakeholders reach consensus on the school district's preferred future vision #2. For our current purposes, *beliefs* and *values* shall be the initial area of the four discussed.

Every individual and every group of people have a collection of beliefs and values that influence what they do. It is crucial to the long-term success of the strategic planning effort that a consensus of the beliefs and values held by the strategic planning stakeholders be arrived at, as these beliefs and values will, in large part, determine the culture that will exist in the district. A few examples will illustrate some beliefs and values:

- All students can learn.
- Emphasis on many decisions that affect individual school buildings and their operations should be made by the employees of each individual school and by the parents of the children who attend that school.
- High achievement levels should be stressed for both students and employees.
- All programs and activities within the school district should include result-based components.

Step two B: This step involves the collection of data related to external variables that may positively or negatively impact the strategic plans of the school district. Once the data are collected over a period of years, trends can be identified that should be accounted for in the strategic plans that are developed [7]. Two examples of external data related to a school district could include: (1) a trend toward a decreasing percent of the total school district supplied by state funds (hard data) and (2) attitudinal surveys of school district residents that indicate an increasingly favorable view of the school district's activities (soft data). Hard data is factual information, and soft data is perceptual or attitudinal information.

Step two C: This step involves collection of data related to the internal aspects of the school district, and trends over a period of time are important sources of information to be taken into account by the strategic planners. Two examples are student achievement scores and student dropout rates.

Step two D: This step involves reaching consensus on those very few items (probably no more than six) that are considered absolutely crucial to the success of a school district. Two examples of CSFs probably will include (1) high level of students' achievement and (2) a conducive school climate.

Step three: Once the four sources of information have been collected and analyzed, the strategic planners should develop their final preferred future vision #2. This vision becomes the planning guide for all further strategic planning activities; and it will include mega (societal), macro (total district), and micro (subunit) elements. It is at this stage where a needs assessment takes place, to identify the elements to be included in the vision and the remaining steps of the strategic plan.

Needs can be defined as gaps or discrepancies between what currently exists and what should or could exist in the future. The purpose of strategic and tactical planning is to eliminate the gaps that exist between what is and what should or could be.

Step four: A mission statement is normally a single sentence that states the central purpose of an organization. In some cases, the single sentence mission is supplemented by a series of statements elaborating upon the mission statement. An example mission statement could well be similar to: "The MISSION of Promising School District is to create a learning environment wherein ALL CHILDREN AND YOUTH shall achieve a learning result that is at the MASTERY level."

Step five: This step is the one at which the strategic planners reach consensus on the goals that provide the *what* directions subsumed under the umbrella of the preferred future vision. An example goal is one that states all students shall achieve a high school diploma. Goals spell out general direction, whereas objectives spell out the specific targets subsumed under each goal.

Tactical Planning Model's Steps

Step six: Once the strategic goals have been decided upon, the next activity is that of conducting an external and an internal S.W.O.T. (strengths, weaknesses, opportunities, and threats) analysis. This step involves analysis of those items that are internal to the school district that might assist or negatively impact the achievement of the strategic goals. The same process is used to isolate those external items that might negatively or positively impact the achievement of the strategic goals [8].

Examples of internal items might include (1) a decreasing pattern of student achievement in mathematics (weakness) or (2) an ever-increasing quality of the employees available to the district (strength).

Examples of external items might include (1) an organized anti-school group (threat) or (2) a large number of retired people in the school district that could be recruited as school volunteers (opportunities).

Step seven: The development of specific objectives, in this case, has been delegated by the strategic planning group to the tactical planners. Tactical planners are normally the employees of the school district, and nonemployee stakeholders are usually not members of the tactical planning group.

Planners cannot quit their work with agreement on strategic goals. They must develop specific objectives for each of the strategic goals that make up the preferred future vision for the school district. An example objective might well be stated as: "The current student high school dropout rate shall be reduced within three years by 20% of the rate that exists today.

Step eight: Often, strategic planners provide too many goals to be reasonably attacked over a five-year or less period of time. Since each of these goals might also include numerous subobjectives, it is crucial to have some method of deciding which goals and objectives should be the priority ones to be dealt with over the five-year time period. The dilemma can be resolved by developing a series of simply stated decision rules. These decision rules might be similar to those listed below:

- The objective should be *achievable.*
- Achievement of the objective should be *affordable.*
- The objective should be *meaningful.*
- The objective should have an 80% *chance of success.*

The 80% (mastery) level is important, as the planners first approach programs to achieve the objectives. That is, the planners must quickly experience success, and it is important that the initial objectives tackled are weighted toward those that have a high probability of successful achievement. Once the planners have experienced sufficient successes, they can then tackle objectives that may be very important but that have a much lower (50% or below) chance of being successfully achieved. Occasional failure to achieve an objective will not negatively influence the planners if they are seasoned planners who have previously experienced much success.

Step nine: Once the decision rules are utilized to select the priority objectives to be attacked, the tactical planners must develop specific action plans. A sequence that is important in the development of comprehensive action plans designed to achieve each specific objective includes four activities: (1) brainstorm alternatives, (2) complete a force field analysis, (3) conduct a cost/benefit analysis, and (4) select the best alternative.

Brainstorming includes quickly developing a comprehensive list of possible action programs that serve as alternative means of achieving a specific objective. Once the brainstorming is included and the most potentially positive suggestions are isolated, a force field analysis should be conducted on each of the possible alternatives.

A force field analysis is an exercise whereby each objective is studied to estimate those factors that will assist and those factors that will constrain the attempts to successfully implement the program designed to achieve the specific objective. An abbreviated example will illustrate this procedure.

Objective: to Initiate a Nursery School Component in the Schools

Supportive Factors	Constraining Factors
1. Working parents want a safe and affordable place for their preschool children.	1. Private preschool owners
2. Many employees have preschool children, and they would appreciate having them in their school.	2. Nonparent taxpayers

A cost/benefit analysis involves determining the ratio of benefits to costs. If the benefits are determined to be greater than the costs, the action program should be implemented. If the costs are greater than the predicted benefits, the action program should not be implemented, and another action program should be considered.

Once the tactical planners have conducted a brainstorming activity, a force field analysis, and a cost/benefit analysis, they are then in an intelligent position to select the best alternative action program designed to meet the specific objective. Once this is done, the planners can allocate resources and plan to operate and manage the selected action plan.

Step ten: In order to allocate resources and operate the selected plan, the detailed answers must be decided upon. The planners have to develop comprehensive answers to the following questions:

• Why should this plan be used?
• What tasks have to be included to cause this plan to be implemented, and what resources shall be allocated to this action program?
• Who is to be held responsible for each task being completed, and who is to be responsible for the desired results?
• When shall the action program take place?
• How will the action program be implemented, and how will the degree of successful achievement be measured?

Steps eleven and twelve: These steps involve monitoring data, analyzing activities and results, and evaluating what has taken place. During the process of operating the action plan, these activities are called *formative evaluation,* and measurement at the end point of terminating of the action plan is called a *summative evaluation.* The tactical planners may find that things aren't working as well as they were designed to work; and, in these cases, the recycling phase is activated.

Once these twelve steps are completed, the resultant information is relayed to the strategic planners, who again initiate the strategic planning process. It is important to stress that both the strategic and tactical planning models include a recycling phase.

Now that the vehicles of strategic and tactical planning are established as the structure within which the other school improvement plans shall be embellished, let's turn to those other specific school improvement structures and processes. We begin with the topic of Total Quality Management.

TOTAL QUALITY MANAGEMENT: THE ULTIMATE QUEST

Total Quality Management has entered the restructuring consider-ations of school district decision makers through the successes witnessed by business and industry in Japan, the United States, and Europe. It is being heavily promoted by the American Association of School Administrators, and many other school related national and state associations are promoting this restructuring program [9]. Awards, like the Deming Award given by Japan and the Baldridge Award presented by the United States to its businesses and industries that meet an extensive list of quality standards, are also heightening the interest among school people [10].

The Total Quality Management movement, sometimes merely called Quality, can provide the guiding quest in a holistic approach to Educational Quality Management. TQM utilizes simple ideas, but it demands a long-term commitment to change and to the development of a more productive organizational culture [11].

The core ideas incorporated within TQM include the following clear conceptual beliefs [12]:

- Quality results are expected for *every service* provided.
- Quality results are expected in *every product* that is delivered.
- *Value is to be added* at every step in the process of developing a service or a product.
- Stakeholders who are to develop the products and deliver the services are to be empowered with decision-making authority.
- Data collection and feedback are continuous.
- Planning is continuous based upon data collection and feedback.
- Customer satisfaction with its product and service is the ultimate challenge.

Now that we have reviewed the key elements of TQM let's turn to an area that can provide guidepoints for strategic goals. Effective Schools Correlates provides such a set of guidepoints.

EFFECTIVE SCHOOLS CORRELATES: GUIDEPOINTS FOR STRATEGIC GOALS

After many years of research, certain characteristics have been iden-tified by researchers to be present in those schools that are considered to be effective in creating an environment that leads to high student achievement levels. These findings are most often called correlates of effective schools. Simply stated, correlative findings indicate that when certain characteristics are present, the school is identified as being effective; and when these characteristics are not present or are not present to a sufficient degree, schools tend to be ineffective.

Correlative research differs from cause-and-effect research, wherein statistically significant proof exists that when a certain variable is introduced, the desired effect or result will occur to a statistically significant degree. Cause-and-effect research is considered to provide more powerful proofs than correlative research. However, in education and in most of the social sciences, correlative research findings have provided important information that could be used in the decision makers' attempts to improve school districts and other social science agencies.

Over the past three decades, researchers have discovered some important characteristics that directly relate to those schools that are considered to be effective. These correlates can be used within the strategic planning structure as part of beliefs, as goals, and as an important element in the preferred future vision of a school district.

The correlates that have been determined to be in existence in effective schools include the following [13]:

- Strong instructional leadership exists in effective schools.
- A safe and orderly school climate conducive to learning exists in effective schools.
- High teacher and administrator expectations for students' achievement exist in effective schools.
- High emphasis is placed on the mastery of basic skills by *all* students in the areas of reading, mathematics, and language arts.
- Regular and continuing feedback on the academic progress of each student is provided in schools that are effective.
- Parent and community involvement is present to a large degree in those schools that are effective.

Now that the potential of the Effective Schools Correlates as an important source of strategic goals to be integrated into a strategic planning process has been reviewed, it is time to turn to a structure that will allow the empowerment of a wide variety of stakeholders to become involved in important decision making at the individual school building level. This involvement will bring greater support for the decisions and activities related to all the goals and activities that are crucial to successfully complete a productive, comprehensive, and high-quality holistic approach to planning.

SCHOOL-BASED MANAGEMENT: AN EMPOWERMENT STRUCTURE

School-Based Management is a restructuring movement that is increasing in popularity. It is championed by a variety of individuals and groups, and in a few states it is mandated by the legislature of the state. Besides a few state legislatures, others involved in promoting SBM include well-known innovators, well-known change agents, many teacher unions, school boards, superintendents of schools, school principals, and various individuals within school districts who wish to change the way school business and design making have been traditionally conducted. It is a dramatic change in the way that most school districts have traditionally operated in that it involves a variety of stakeholders in decision making who have not been traditionally empowered to make decisions, and it delegates a variety of decision-making authority that has been traditionally held by the central school district's decision makers to those stakeholders who are empowered to make decisions related to the local school building's operation [14].

School-Based Management commitees always include teachers and the school principal, often involve parents, and sometimes involve students and nonparent community representatives. Those persons serving on SBM committees often have decision-making authority over many budgetary and instructional areas; and sometimes the SBM committees are given decision-making authority in areas of personnel, student services, local school policy, and matters related to local school governance. Also, in most cases, the local SBM committees are provided with an appeals process that can be used to request an exemption from any board of education policy [15].

The keys to success of this restructuring program are four in number: (1) the board, the superintendent of schools, and the administrators must be in support of this movement; (2) a sufficient number of elected or voluntary SBM committee members have to be willing to put in a great deal of time and effort to make this approach successful; (3) a clear set of decisions on the various areas of decision-making authority between the central and building levels have to be made prior to implementation of the SBM program; and (4) sufficient training of the participants must be conducted prior to the beginning of the SBM activities, and this training should be continued once the SBM structure and processes are implemented.

Now that the empowerment element of SBM has been identified, let's turn to the matter of Outcome-Based Education as a measurement technique. OBE should also become an integral part of the holistic approach to Educational Quality Management.

OUTCOME-BASED EDUCATION: A MEASUREMENT TECHNIQUE

Outcome-Based Education is based on the premise that *all* students can learn, and it uses a definition of mastery as a measurement tool. Mastery generally means that each student will prove achievement of at least 80% of criterion measurement items or norm-referenced items used to measure the student's degree of learning [16].

OBE is also outcome or results driven, and it generally uses criterion-based student assessments. It is based on data collection, feedback, and recycling process, if mastery is not achieved.

Finally, it usually believes that a supportive educational climate must exist to assist the students to achieve at a mastery level. This supportive climate includes teachers who hold high expectations for each student and who believe that each student can learn, and it involves a Management Information System (MIS) that continually collects and monitors students' achievement data that is fed back to the teachers and students. This feedback is then used to provide specific instructional delivery methods and information designed to assist each student to achieve mastery learning [17].

MODEL OF A POWERFUL, SYSTEMATIC, AND INTEGRATED OPERATING SYSTEM FOR SCHOOLS

If any school district's decision makers are interested in attempting to improve their school district and its component schools, they would be wise to first assess the organization's readiness for change, and next develop a holistic approach to school improvement by using the best of all the various restructuring and school improvement programs that are currently in vogue. This approach, for purposes of this discussion, is called Educational Quality Management [18–20].

Once the school district's decision makers feel that the school district is in a position to attempt systematic, transformational change, they can address the task of articulating the various programs of Total Quality Management, Outcome-Based Education, Effective Schools research, School-Based Management, strategic planning, and tactical planning into an integrated holistic approach [21–23].

An uncomplicated model, such as that presented in Figure 10.3, can graphically illustrate how TQM, Effective Schools, OBE, SBM, strategic planning, and tactical planning can be integrated into a holistic approach to school improvement.

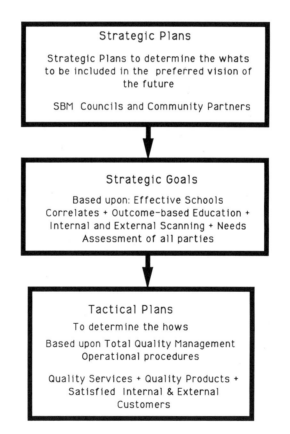

Figure 10.3. Tying TQM, Effective Schools Research, strategic planning, tactical planning, Outcome-Based Education, and School-Based Management together.

DESIGNING A HOLISTIC APPROACH TO EDUCATIONAL QUALITY MANAGEMENT

When reviewing the key concepts of OBE, SBM, TQM, Effective Schools, strategic planning, and tactical planning, we discover that a complementary approach to these concepts permits the development of a holistic approach to positive systematic and transformational change in schools [27,28]. The total array of the key concepts for each of these numerous approaches is presented in Figure 10.4. In addition, the interface between and among these key concepts and planning steps is displayed in Figure 10.5.

Finally, the holistic Matrix, displayed in Figure 10.6, proves that, by using strategic and tactical planning concepts as the basic structural means of developing a holistic approach that includes all currently favored restructuring and school improvement approaches, it is possible and profitable to unite the concepts of OBE, SBM, TQM, and Effective Schools with the strategic and tactical planning concepts [29, 30]. It is clear that, almost uniformly, each step of the strategic and tactical planning structures and processes can accommodate the concepts of OBE, TQM, SBM, and Effective Schools. It is very clear that *strong evidence* exists to prove the commonality, in most programs, of the concepts of the following [31–33]:

- empowerment
- needs assessment
- goals
- objectives
- action programs
- data collection and feedback
- recycling phase
- planning
- strong leadership
- collaborative decision making
- conducive support climate

It is important that those who are responsible for wise decision making at the school district or school building level understand that it makes a great deal of sense to locate the common elements in each popular plan for school improvement, rather than using, as independent programs, each of the popular restructuring and school improvement programs of (1) Outcome-Based Education, (2) Total Quality

---

TOTAL QUALITY MANAGEMENT

1. Vision of continual improving quality
2. Quality goals
3. Value added concept of quality at each juncture
4. Quality results in products and services

5. Empowers stakeholders
6. Planning is continuous
7. Data collection and feedback
8. Customer satisfaction

OUTCOME-BASED EDUCATION

1. ALL students can learn
2. Mastery concept
3. Outcome/results driven
4. Criterion-based Assessment
5. Data collection and feedback - MIS (management information system)
6. High achievement expectations
7. Supportive educational climate

EFFECTIVE SCHOOLS

1. Vision of what should be (preferred future vision)
2. Strong instructional leadership
3. Safe and orderly climate conducive to learning
4. High expectations for achievement
5. Emphasis on mastery of basic skills
6. Regular and continuous feedback on academic progress
7. Parent and community involvement

SCHOOL-BASED MANAGEMENT

1. Authority and accountability shifted to school site level (empowerment shift)
2. Collaborative decision making is the process used
3. Stakeholders are involved in school site decision making
4. A conducive support climate exists

Figure 10.4. Key planning concepts.

Management, (3) School-Based Management, (4) Effective Schools, (5) strategic planning, and (6) tactical planning as independent methodologies when attempting to improve the school district or its component schools.

In fact, if more than one of these current restructuring and school improvement programs are attempted at the same time in any school district or school building, without coordinating the elements of each into a singular approach, conflict between or among the various approaches could result in immediate and permanent damage. Again, if the initial efforts of an uncoordinated approach result in failure, it will be a very long time before the district's or school building's stakeholders will be willing to put in the time or expend their efforts on another restructuring or school improvement scheme.

At this juncture, we can turn our attention to an example that utilizes this holistic approach to restructuring and school improvements. The

PLANNING STEPS

STRATEGIC PLAN

A. Vision
B. Beliefs and values
C. External and Internal Scanning
D. Critical Success Factors
E. Needs assessment
F. Mission
G. SWOT Analysis
H. Strategic goals
I. Specific objectives for goals
J. Evaluate and recycle

TACTICAL PLAN

K. Decision rules to determine priorities

L. Action plans:
    (a) Brainstorm
    (b) Force field Analysis
    (c) Cost/benefit Analysis
    (d) Select best alternative
    (e) Allocate resources and
        operate plans

M. Evaluate and recycle

KEY CONCEPTS

Total QUALITY MANAGEMENT

1. Vision
2. Goals
3. Empowerment
4. Continuous planning
5. Data collection and feedback
6. Value added at each juncture
7. Quality results (services and products)
8. Customer satisfaction

EFFECTIVE SCHOOLS

1. Vision of preferred future
2. Instructional leadership
3. Parent and community involvement
4. Conducive climate
5. Emphasis on basic skills – mastery
6. Data collection and feedback
7. High achievement expectations

SCHOOL–BASED MANAGEMENT

1. Empowerment to the school site
2. Stakeholders' involvement in decisions
3. Collaborative decision making
4. Conducive support climate

OUTCOME–BASED EDUCATION

1. ALL students can learn
2. Mastery concept
3. Outcome/results driven
4. High achievement expectations
5. Criterion-based assessment
6. Data collection and feedback
7. Supportive educational climate

Figure 10.5. Interface between key concepts and planning steps.

DIRECTIONS: Place a large X when the characteristic is an absolute, and place a small x when the characteristic is applicable but not absolute.

KEY CHARACTERISTICS	OBE	SBM	TQM	EFF SCHS	STRAT &TACT PLANNING
STRATEGIC & TACTICAL PLANNING					
1. Vision	x	x	x	x	X
2. Empowered stakeholders	—	X	X	X	X
3. Needs assessment	X	X	X	X	X
4. Goals	X	X	X	X	X
5. Objectives	X	X	X	X	X
6. Action programs	X	X	X	X	X
7. Data collection and feedback	X	X	X	X	X
8. Recycling	X	X	X	X	X
TOTAL QUALITY MANAGEMENT					
1. Vision & goals	X	x	X	x	x
2. Quality products & services results	X	x	X	X	X
3. Value added at each juncture	X	x	X	x	x
4. Empowered stakeholders	—	X	X	X	X
5. Data collection and feedback	X	X	X	X	X
6. Customer satisfaction	x	x	X	x	x
7. Continuous Planning	X	X	X	X	X
EFFECTIVE SCHOOLS:					
1. Strong leadership	X	X	X	X	X
2. Safe and orderly climate	X	x	x	X	x
3. High achievement expectations	X	x	X	X	X
4. Mastery	X	x	x	X	x
5. Data collection and feedback	X	X	X	X	X
6. Parents and community involved	—	X	x	X	X
7. Vision of preferred future	x	x	x	x	X
SCHOOL-BASED MANAGEMENT:					
1. Site level decision making	X	X	X	X	x
2. Empowered stakeholders	—	X	X	X	X
3. Collaborative decision making	—	X	X	X	X
4. Conducive support climate	X	X	X	X	X

Figure 10.6. Holistic matrix for systematic transformational change.

KEY CHARACTERISTICS	OBE	SBM	TQM	EFF SCHS	STRAT &TACT PLANNING
OUTCOME-BASED EDUCATION					
1. ALL students can learn	X	——	x	X	X
2. Mastery concept	X	——	X	X	x
3. Outcome/results driven	X	x	X	X	X
4. High achievement expectations	X	X	X	X	X
5. Criterion-based assessment	X	x	X	x	X
6. Data collection and feedback	X	X	X	X	X
7. Supportive educational climate	X	X	X	X	X

Figure 10.6 (continued). Holistic matrix for systematic transformational change.

hypothetical Wonderful School District will be used to illustrate this matter.

THEORY-TO-PRACTICE EXAMPLE

The following is an example of a model for a powerful, systematic, and integrated system for schools.

WONDERFUL SCHOOL DISTRICT'S HOLISTIC EDUCATIONAL QUALITY MANAGEMENT EXAMPLE

The board of education, the superintendent of schools, the teachers' union, and the district's administrators all agree that a new method of improving the school district and the component schools is required; and they realize that to accomplish this, much planning has to take place and a wide variety of stakeholders have to be supportive of the activities. These decision makers agree to organize a stakeholders' steering committee that would be oriented to and trained in the techniques used by strategic planners. At the same time, a core group of employees would be oriented to and trained in the techniques used by tactical planners.

In addition, both groups would be provided with information and training in the restructuring and school improvement programs of (1) Outcome-Based Education, (2) School-Based Management, (3) Total Quality Management, and (4) Effective Schools. Eventually, the core stakeholders' strategic planning committee and the core employees' tactical planning committee were asked to complete a unified holistic plan that utilized the key concepts from all of these programs and to relate this holistic structure and its processes to an improvement model for Wonderful School District [34,35].

The stakeholders' strategic planning committee drew its membership from parents, community representatives, teachers, students, classified employees, building-level administrators, and central office administrators. The core employees' tactical planning committee drew its membership from teachers, classified employees, building-level administrators, and central office administrators.

The results of the efforts of both the stakeholders' strategic planning committee and its subcommittees and of the core employees' tactical planning committee and its subcommittees are listed below. It should be stressed that these results were the results of collaborative efforts, and decisions were arrived at through consensus techniques.

Vision #1

The members of the stakeholders' strategic planning committee spent much time discussing a scenario that included all indicators of what they would like their school district and component schools to look like within five to ten years. This vision included students' achievement levels, parent and community participation, employees' contributions, and many other indicators to be included in the preferred future vision. Having reached consensus on this initial preferred future vision, the strategic planning committee members decided that they had better collect much information and then determine if this initial vision should be modified when faced with the information collected.

Beliefs and Values

The committee agreed that its initial task was to reach consensus on the beliefs and values that would guide the remainder of the planning process. For they knew that, if a conflict in beliefs and values existed, further planning progress would be greatly impeded. Some of the core beliefs and values agreed to include the following:

- All students, N–12, or adult students, can learn.
- The school district and its component schools are part of a broader society, and they should participate in meeting certain societal needs. A need is a gap or discrepancy between what is and what should or could be.
- All students, employees, parents, and citizens should be thought of as internal or external customers of the school district; and they should be treated as valued customers by the employees of the school district.
- Parents, community members, students, teachers, administrators, and classified employees should be given important roles in the decisions of the district, especially those related to the school building site level and to the specific employee's job.
- Detailed and continuous planning is a necessary ingredient to successful schools.
- Schools should be outcome/results based.
- Data collected should be both of the hard (factual) variety and of the soft (perceptual) variety.
- An MIS should be in place to monitor, assess, and evaluate all activities and results.

External Scanning

Once the committee reached consensus on its statement of beliefs and values, it collected and scanned data to determine the positive and negative trends that existed in the school district's external environment. This was important, as the positive trends can assist the district in attaining its preferred future vision; and the negative trends serve as warning signals to be avoided, nullified, or minimized. A few *external trends* will demonstrate the external scanning findings:

- The school district has continually become more multicultural in nature over the past ten years, and this trend is likely to continue.
- Over 50% of the students come from single-family homes, and another 22% have both parents working outside the home. This is a long-term trend and will predictably continue for the next five to ten years.

- New businesses continue to locate in the school district, and this provides a much increased tax base to assist in the financial support of the school district.

Internal Scanning

A few of the *internal trends* that were discovered included the following:

- The students in the high school have an increasing dropout rate pattern. The current dropout rate exceeds 24%.
- Employees' attitudinal surveys indicate an increasing positive attitude by the employees as a group. The total favorable responses equal 85%, but the custodial workers indicate only a 28% favorable response.

Critical Success Factors

Once the scanning was completed, the stakeholders' strategic planning committee was determined to identify those few factors that were absolutely critical to the future success of the school district and to the achievement of the preferred future vision. After three months of discussion and deliberations, the committee finally arrived at the following list of factors that they considered critical:

- All students should graduate from high school, and they should become productive citizens. A productive citizen is one who produces more than she/he consumes.
- Each student should achieve mastery on the learning outcomes that are appropriate for her/him.
- Internal and external customer satisfaction with the products and services of the schools is crucial to success.
- Many employee, student, and community stakeholders should be involved in the decision-making structures and processes of the school district, as this is the means of gathering a critical mass of support for the schools, their programs, and their actvities.
- Strategic and tactical planning are obligatory activities.

Vision #2

Based upon the information collected and upon the needs discovered by the committee's assessment of the mega (societal) needs, the macro (total district) needs, and the micro (building level and other subunit) needs, the stakeholders' strategic planning committee arrived at its vision #2; and this vision then served as the guideline for all further strategic planning activities. Vision #2 made some modification in the initial vision upon which the committee members previously reached consensus.

Mission Statement

Having arrived at its operational vision, the stakeholders' strategic planning committee began the task of developing a single sentence mission statement. After much discussion and numerous ideas and debates, the following mission statement was adopted: The MISSION of Wonderful School District is to produce high-achieving students who will become productive society members, and the district will strive to continuously improve the products and services it delivers to all of its external and internal customers.

Strategic Goals

Once the stakeholders' strategic planning committee finalized Wonderful School District's mission statement, the members turned to the task of developing strategic goals that fell within the umbrella of the preferred future vision and the mission of the school district. The strategic goals the committee members agreed upon, in part, are listed below:

- *All* students can learn, and each student is expected to attain a mastery level of what is taught.
- Students, teachers, and administrators will hold high achievement expectations.
- A safe and nurturing environment will be provided for both students and employees.
- Everyone internal to the schools and external to the schools will be thought of as valued customers to be treated with the same courtesies and respect that the employees and students desire for themselves.
- The schools will become results oriented; and an MIS will be developed to monitor, analyze, and evaluate the degree to which the results attained match those desired.

- Collaborative, consensual, and school site–based decision making will become the norm.
- The school district will be seen as part of the broader community and society, and mega (societal) goals shall join macro (total school district) goals and micro (school building or other subunit) goals as important elements in the strategic and tactical planning activities of Wonderful School District.
- Strategic and tactical planning will become continuing activities.
- A value-added approach to the development and delivery of the products and the services provided by Wonderful School District will become the S.O.P. (standard operating procedure).
- The final outcome of all of the other strategic goals shall be the production of well-educated high school graduates who will become productive citizens. A productive citizen is one who produces more than she or he consumes.

Specific Objectives

For each strategic goal, one or many subobjectives may be developed. Each objective should be stated in clear-results terms that can be measured and evaluated. A couple of examples will illustrate this next step.

(1) *Objective #1:* Within two years, the student high school dropout rate will be reduced by 8%; and within five years, the total dropout rate for all high school students will be less than 2% per year.

(2) Objective *#2:* Within one year, a School-Based Management committee will be operational within a minimum of one elementary school, one middle school, and one senior high school. Within five years, a School-Based Management committee will be operational in all schools within Wonderful School District. This shall result in a minimum of 51% of the district's residents and employees becoming a part of the decision-making, accountability, and communication structures of the school district.

Internal and External S.W.O.T. Analyses

Once the stakeholders' strategic planning committee has identified and reached consensus on the strategic goals and specific objectives to be accomplished, they completed an internal and external S.W.O.T.

(strengths, weaknesses, opportunities, and threats) analysis to determine those variables that would prove helpful to meeting the established goals and objectives and to also determine those variables that might prove hindrances to meeting the established goals and objectives.

The presentation of two external and two internal variables will illustrate this procedure. The purpose of this analysis is to capitalize on the identified strengths and opportunities to eliminate or reduce the impact of the threats, and to correct all identified weaknesses.

Internal S.W.O.T. Analysis' Findings

(1) High employee and student morale will assist in achieving the desired goals and objectives (internal strength).
(2) An increasing student dropout rate appears to be continuing (internal weakness).

External S.W.O.T. Analysis' Findings

(1) There are a large number of well-educated retired residents living within Wonderful School District, many of whom have expressed an interest in becoming volunteers to the schools of the district (external opportunity).
(2) There is a declining pattern of federal and state financial aid to the school district (external threat).

Decision Rules

Having analyzed the external and internal S.W.O.T. variables, the members of the stakeholders' strategic planning committee realized that they had too much on their action plate. That is, they had too many goals and objectives to be meaningfully dealt with over the next five-year period. Therefore, they decided to develop some simple decision rules to assist them in assigning priorities to all the strategic goals and specific objectives. When the prioritizations were completed, the strategic and tactical planners would be faced with a reasonable number of activities to pursue over the next five-year period. The simply stated screening rules they decided upon were:

- The goal or objective had to be *affordable* in terms of time, people, and financial resources.

- The goal or objective had to be results based, and it had to be clearly *achievable.*
- The goal or objective had to end in a *meaningful* result.

Utilizing the decision rules that they had decided upon, the stakeholders' strategic planning committee decided to turn the remainder of the planning over to those administrators, teachers, and other school employees who were to be held accountable for developing tactical action plans designed to achieve the strategic goals and specific objectives outlined by the stakeholders' strategic planning committee. But the stakeholders' committee recommended that a tactical planning progress report be provided at the regularly called monthly board of education meeting and that the tactical planning committee provide a quarterly written and oral report to the stakeholders' strategic planning committee.

The employees who comprised the tactical planning committee began their development of action plans by carrying out four exercises that included: (1) brainstorming possible alternative action plans, (2) conducting a force field analysis of the potentially most promising action plans, (3) conducting a cost/benefit analysis of each potentially promising action plan, and (4) selecting the best alternative action plan based upon the three previous analyses.

Brainstorming

Brainstorming was conducted using a specific set of brainstorming rules to generate as many ideas as possible within a very short time period. The tactical planners generated eighty-five ideas within twelve minutes as they addressed a single objective. The brainstorming rules developed and utilized by the tactical planners were:

- *All* ideas are encouraged.
- There is to be no discussion of any idea.
- There is to be no explanation of any idea presented.
- Piggybacking on another's idea is acceptable and encouraged.
- There is to be no verbal or nonverbal expression of approval or disapproval of any idea presented.

Force-Field Analysis

Using the stated objective of having School-Based Management committees functioning in every school within the school district in a period of five years, we can complete a hypothetical force-field analysis.

Supporting Factors	Constraining Factors
1. Many teachers favor the creation of SBM committees.	1. Some teachers oppose the creation of SBM committees.
2. Parents and citizens are given a bigger voice in how the school is run.	2. The board of education and the superintendent are uneasy about delegating much of their decision-making authority.
3. This approach will ultimately bring much greater community support for the schools.	3. Some principals are absolutely opposed to having parents tell them how to run their schools; they don't want to be held accountable for group decisions.
4. The teachers' union is supportive of this.	4. Many teachers are willing to spend additional time without additional pay.
5. This approach has proven successful in many areas of the United States.	5. It is dangerous to provide decision power to a group whose members are not experienced in educational matters or group consensus decision making.
6. Other (specify)	6. Other (specify)

Cost/Benefit Analysis

Many times a cost/benefit analysis of a proposed action program is also required. This type of analysis merely lists the actual cost of the proposed action program and then compares the cost to the anticipated benefits. If the cost is greater than the anticipated benefits, the proposed action program is not operationalized. If the benefits are predicted to be greater than the cost, then the action program is initiated.

Selection of the Best Alternative Action Program

Once the force-field analysis and the cost/benefit analysis of the proposed action programs have been completed, and the specific program(s) to become operational has been decided upon, the tactical planners turn to the function of listing all of the subtasks involved in bringing the action program to fruition. A simple, but work-intensive, format is helpful. A model format is present below:

Detailed Action Planning Format.

Tasks	Chronology	Person(s) Responsible	Time Target	Resources	Measures of Results

Once the program has been operational, data is collected, analyzed, evaluated, and decisons are made as to the degree of successful achievement of the results desired related to each specific objective and each strategic goal. This information, in turn, is evaluated as to the extent the action program fell within the mission statement and its impact on achieving the ultimate preferred future vision for the Wonderful School District.

After the evaluation has been completed, a decision is made to drop the action program, try it again with modifications, or incorporate it into the S.O.P.s of the school district. Also, once the tactical planners have completed their tasks, whatever the final results, the information is then returned to the stakeholders' strategic planning committee to begin recycling the process. The stakeholders' committee also reviews its (1) beliefs and values statements, (2) external and internal scanning data, (3) CSEs; and, next, the committee members determine whether or not their vision, mission, strategic goals, and specific objectives are still valid and whether or not required modifications are indicated. At this stage, the entire process was renewed for possible modifications.

Final Words

What has been suggested in these pages is that a holistic and coordinated approach that is inclusive of all of the currently proposed restructuring and school improvement programs is the desired method of use for school districts and individual schools. This in no way should be considered foolproof methodology, nor should this be considered a quick-fix method of improving schools. Rather, it is a model that holds great promise of the attainment for the goals of the schools—that of turning out high-quality graduates who will become productive citizens and of providing all of the internal and external customers of the schools with high-quality services and products that they can perceive as satisfactory outputs and outcomes [36,37].

ENABLING BEHAVIORS AND BRIDGES TO NEW PRACTICE

The preceding chapters' sections on the training and staff development facilitations required to adopt or implement the innovation or process described in each can be considered as a continuous strand of recommended bridging strategies required to achieve a holistic quality transformation. The many restructuring ideas that have been suggested, taken as a whole, present a substantial challenge for school districts, implying major cultural change and a long-term commitment for the improvement of our schools and school districts. It is crucial that the local decision makers study these carefully for (1) their individual worth and potential for quality improvement in the schools and (2) their possibility of being integrated with other promising subsets of a holistic transformational and systematic change model that is designed to restructure and improve the quality of our schools.

The keys to successfully implementing and maintaining a holistic transformational change are many, but the main ones include the following [38]:

- Stakeholders must be involved in the process and in the decisions.
- Strategic and operational (tactical) plans must be identified and carried out by the decision makers and the managers of change, and these plans must be aligned.
- A vision, goals, and objectives that spell out the various levels of desired results must be clear and understood by all.
- Data must be collected and analyzed, and feedback must be provided to the decision makers and to the managers of change in

order that they make improvements and modifications as required over time.

- Employees and a critical mass of the other stakeholders must believe in the preferred future vision for the school district and its constituent schools; and they must accept ownership of the strategic goals, specific objectives, and tactical plans that are designed to achieve the preferred future vision.
- The preferred future vision must be one that includes continuous improvement of the quality of the products and services of the school district and its constituent schools. Once this result is attained, the district will witness a mass of satisfied internal and external customers.
- The individual components of Effective Schools, School-Based Management, and Outcome-Based Education must be seen as operating within and informing and guiding the strategic and tactical planning process—creating a holistic, quality-driven method of improving schools.

SUMMARY

This chapter has focused on Educational Quality Management as an integrating catalyst for change, an umbrella concept that has the conceptual and practice-driven capacity to incorporate recommended restructuring components into its dynamics and essential structures. An extensive strategic and tactical planning model was presented in steps that illustrated the procedures and connections between the two processes. Total Quality Management was described as the ultimate restructuring quest to be attained; its core ideas were listed. The Effective Schools Correlates were presented as guidepoints for the development of strategic goals and objectives, forming part of the beliefs and contributing to the preferred future vision of a school district. School-Based Management was presented as an empowerment structure that facilitates the decision-making and stakeholder-involvement characteristics of the planning process. Outcome-Based Education was recommended as a powerful measurement technique, an assessment structure that will provide ongoing information for continuous improvement. A recommendation for the facilitating training needed to assist this implementation was included; and a theory-to-practice example of a model for a powerful, systemic, and integrated system for schools outlined and traced a districts's implementation of holistic school improvement.

PRACTICAL EXERCISES

(1) Outline how you would go about initiating an integrated Quality Management program in your district.
(2) Determine the categories of training and staff development that would be required to facilitate such a program.
(3) Determine the measures and means you would use to evaluate the effectiveness of your Quality Management program.
(4) Describe what you and your organization would have to do to equal or exceed the best organizations in your field of work.

REFERENCES

1. Holzman, M. 1993. "What Is Systemic Change?" *Educational Leadership,* 51(1):18.
2. Wagner, T. 1993. "Systemic Change: Rethinking the Purpose of School," *Educational Leadership,* 51(1):24–28.
3. Herman, J. J. 1993. *Holistic Quality: Managing, Restructuring, Empowering Schools,* Newbury Park, CA: Corwin Press, Inc., a Sage Publications Company.
4. Herman, J. J. and J. L. Herman. In press. *Making Change Happen.* Newbury Park, CA: Corwin Press, Inc., a Sage Publications Company.
5. Kaufman, R. and J. J. Herman. 1991. *Strategic Planning in Education.* Lancaster, PA: Technomic Publishing Company, Inc., p. 246.
6. Herman, J. J. and J. L. Herman. 1993. *School-Based Management: Current Thinking and Practice.* Springfield, IL: Charles C. Thomas, Publisher, Inc., pp. 228–230.
7. Herman, J. J. and G. Megiveron. 1993. *Collective Bargaining in Education: Win/Win, Win/Lose, Lose/Lose.* Lancaster, PA: Technomic Publishing Company, Inc.
8. Herman, J. J. and J. L. Herman. 1991. *The Positive Development of Human Resources and School District Organizations.* Lancaster, PA: Technomic Publishing Company, Inc., pp. 19–20.
9. Levinson, H. J. and C. Dehont. 1992. "Leading to Quality," *Quality Progress,* 25(5):55–60.
10. Peregrine, P. 1993. "Total Quality Assessment Programs for Schools," paper presented at the *Annual Meeting of the American Association of School Administrators,* Orlando, Florida, February 1993.

11. Anderson, B. L. 1993. "The Stages of Systemic Change," *Educational Leadership,* 51(1):14–17.

12. Bragar, J. 1992. "The Customer-Focused Quality Leader," *Quality Progress,* 25(5):51–54.

13. Herman and Herman, 1993, pp. 228–230.

14. Herman, J. J. and J. L. Herman. 1992. *School-Based Management*

15. Herman, J. J. 1992. "Key Steps to Develop School Governance Teams," *The School Administrator,* 49(1):34–35.

16. Zlatos, B. 1993. "Outcomes-Based Outrage," *Executive Educator,* 15(9):12–16.

17. Rubin, S. E. and W. G. Spady. 1984. "Achieving Excellence through Outcome-Based Instructional Delivery,"*Educational Leadership,* 41(8):37–44.

18. Chaudron, D. 1992. "HR and TQM: All Aboard!" *HR Focus,* 69(11):1–6.

19. Levinson and Dehont, pp.55–60.

20. Rhodes, L. A. 1990. "Beyond Your Beliefs: Quantum Leaps Toward Quality Schools," *School Administrator,* 47(10):23–26.

21. Barrow, J. W. 1993. "Does Total Quality Management Equal Organizational Learning?" *Quality Progress,* 26(7):39–44.

22. Siu-Runyon, Y. and S. J. Heart. 1992. "The Management Manifesto," *Executive Educator,* 14(1):23–26.

23. Schmoker, M. and R. B. Wilson. 1993. "Transforming Schools through Total Quality Education," *Phi Delta Kappan,* 74(5):389–395.

24. Evans, R. 1993. "The Human Face of Reform," *Educational Leadership,* 51(1):19–23.

25. Lasher, G. C. 1993. "Quality Schools on a Shoestring," *Thrust for Educational Leadership,* 22(4):8–12.

26. Byrnes, L. 1993. "Creating World-Class Teacher Education Programs with TQM," *TQM in Higher Education,* 2(1):1–2.

27. Gray, R., N. Hobar, R. Gagrys and C. Zimmerman. 1992. *The Total Quality Educator: Adapting Total Quality Management to Education,* Vol. 1 of the *Total Quality Education Trilogy.* Cockeysville, MD: Workforce 2000, Inc.

28. Willis, S. 1993. "Creating 'Total Quality' Schools," *Association of Supervision and Curriculum Development Update,* 35(2):1, 4–5.

29. Fields, J. C. 1993. "Unlocking the Paralysis of Will: Leaders Can Use School Efficacy to Unleash a 'Can-Do' Spirit," *Educational Leadership,* 50(5): 9–13.

30. Betts, F. 1992. "How Systems Thinking Applies to Education," *Educational Leadership,* 50(3):38–41.

31. Duden, N. 1993. "A Move from Effective to Quality," *School Administrator,* 50(5):18–21.

32. Smith, C. A. 1992. "Teams Building Teams: TQM and Classified Personnel Selection," *School Business Affairs,* 58(11):27–29.

33. Hixson, J. and K. Lovelace. 1992. "Total Quality Management's Challenge to Urban Schools," *Educational Leadership,* 50(3):24–27.

34. Schmoker, M. and R. B. Wilson. 1993. "Adapting Total Quality Doesn't Mean 'Turning Learning into a Business,' " *Educational Leadership,* 51(1):62–63.

35. Schenkat, R. 1993. "Deming's Quality: Our Last but Best Hope," *Educational Leadership,* 51(1):64–65.

36. Smith, A. K. 1993. "Total Quality Management in the Public Sector, Part 1," *Quality Progress,* 26(6):45–50.
37. Smith, A. K. 1993. "Total Quality Management in the Public Sector, Part 2," *Quality Progress,* 26(7):57–64.
38. Ibid.

CHAPTER 11

Tying It All Together and Projecting the Future of Educational Quality Management in Schools

THIS chapter discusses (1) advantages of an integrated approach to change and restructuring; (2) potential for systemic, long-term, positive change; and (3) projecting the future of Educational Quality Management (EQM) in schools. It links the previous chapters' theories, models, and proposed implementations with the broad concept of Educational Quality Management.

ADVANTAGES OF AN INTEGRATED APPROACH TO CHANGE AND RESTRUCTURING

The advantages related to an integrated approach to change and restructuring include the facts that: (1) a holistic quality approach will avoid an attempt to unthinkingly implement every restructuring idea that is recommended; (2) it will unify and focus all individual and organizational efforts toward a clear vision, goals, objectives, and series of action programs; (3) it will avoid overlap and conflict among the various restructuring programs being attempted; (4) change will take place on the basis of data collection, analysis, feedback, and recycling activities; and (5) employees and other stakeholders will understand that a well-planned, holistic approach to school improvement is being initiated by the school district and its constituent schools; and they will also be assured as to what aspects of the organization will remain unaltered and what will be changed [1,2].

Although there are many advantages to change and restructuring, there are some cautions that must be stressed. These include: (1) causing holistic transformational and systemic change is much more complicated than merely integrating a single restructuring idea into an existing operational structure; (2) implementing a holistic, transformational, and systematic change is a long-term, working, and thinking-intensive activity, and many individuals may not be able to meet this comprehensive challenge; and (3) a holistic, transformational, and systemic change is a continuing, never-ending process; and the quest for continual quality improvement may be difficult to maintain as individuals change, as new people enter the employment of the school district, and as future promising restructuring ideas have to be integrated into this holistic approach [3,4].

POTENTIAL FOR SYSTEMATIC, LONG-TERM POSITIVE CHANGE

Educational Quality Management (EQM) involves transformational change that, when completed, will redesign the current planning structures and processes utilized in the school district and/or the school building. Ultimately, the successful implementation of Total Quality Management (TQM) will lead to a new organizational culture that will produce high-quality results and a great degree of customer satisfaction [5,6].

Regardless of which of the approaches to improvement are used (Quality Management, School-Based Management, Outcome-Based Education, Effective Schools, or strategic and tactical planning), change is involved. Whether that change becomes only cosmetic, whether it becomes a true systemic transformational change, and whether it becomes a short-term or a long-term change depend on many variables: ownership by a critical mass of stakeholders and believers; adequate fiscal, temporal, and human resources; and a long-term view aimed at achieving a vision of what should be [7,8]. Systemic change must focus on two organizational aspects: (1) the restructuring must *simultaneously focus* on the development and on the *interrelationships of all the main components* of the system, and (2) the restructuring must focus on *structure, process, and culture,* simultaneously.

If a school district or an individual school is to be transformationally and systemically changed and if that process is to create a culture that results in dramatic changes in the structures, processes, and attitudes that exist in the organization, it has a much better opportunity to do these things if it unifies and blends the separate approaches into one coordinated and complementary approach to transformational change, and to a new systemic organizational culture [9].

It would be wise for the school district's or individual school building's decision makers to assess their organization's potential and receptivity for change prior to attempting the individual, and possibly disjointed, change procedures of QM, SBM, OBE, Effective Schools, or strategic and tactical planning. If the decision makers are going to attempt transformational change, which involves the integration of the individual change programs into one holistic and systemic change structure and process, they should always assess the organization's (which means the employees' and other stakeholders') readiness prior to initiating the change effort. In this way, they can capitalize on the positive support areas and work to overcome the areas of resistance [10].

Once the decision makers feel that the organization is sufficiently ready to attempt systemic, transformational change, they can begin the task of integrating the various programs of QM, SBM, OBE, Effective Schools, and strategic and tactical planning into a holistic structure to achieve true systemic change. Chapter 10 described how these various programs fit within a holistic model. Considering that demonstrated overlap and commonality of concept, it should be clear that it makes sense to plan holistically. In fact, if more than one of these current restructuring efforts are attempted in the same school district or same school building without integrating them into a single approach effort, conflict between, or among, the various restructuring methods could result in much damage [11]. Also, if the initial efforts at restructuring are unsuccessful because of the lack of coordination between, or among, the various methods, it will be a very long time before stakeholders will be willing to accept another restructuring approach or to put their efforts into any change strategy.

PROJECTING THE FUTURE OF EQM IN SCHOOLS

TQM is being implemented in more and more organizations each year. With some modifications to the model employed in the industrial and business sectors, TQM does offer an inviting restructuring opportunity for educators to explore [12].

Many innovative programs and means have been suggested as restructuring ideas that will improve our schools. It is crucial that the local decision makers carefully consider these for (1) their individual worth and potential for quality improvement in the schools and (2) their possibility of being integrated with other promising subsets of a holistic transformational and systematic change model [13].

The keys to successfully implementing and maintaining a holistic transformational change that will result in a viable educational quality system are many, but chiefly include the following [14–16]:

- Stakeholders must be involved in the process and in the decisions.
- Strategic and operational (tactical) plans must be identified and carried out by the decision makers and the managers of change, and these plans must be aligned.
- A vision, goals, and objectives that spell out the various levels of desired results must be clear and understood by all.
- Data must be collected and analyzed, and feedback must be provided to the decision makers and to the managers of change in order that they make improvements and modifications as required over time.
- Employees and a critical mass of other stakeholders must believe in the preferred future vision for the school district and its constituent schools; and they must accept ownership of the strategic goals, specific objectives, and tactical plans that are designed to achieve the preferred future vision.
- The preferred future vision must be one that includes continuous improvement of the quality of the products and services of the school district and its constituent schools. Once this result is attained, the district will have a mass of satisfied internal and external customers.

What is suggested here is not an immediate and foolproof method of improving schools. It is, instead, a long-term planning approach that integrates the various most popular current restructuring ideas into a holistic approach to Educational Quality Management. It avoids conflicts among the various suggested approaches, and it holds great promise for attaining the ultimate goals—that of turning out high-quality graduates who will become productive citizens and providing all of the schools' customers with high-quality services and products. In so doing, EQM offers the outcomes of

- a high level of both internal and external customer satisfaction
- a system of continuous and accurate two-way communications and feedback within and outside of the organization

- a collaborative and empowering environment for all categories of the school's or school district's customers, particularly, students and employees
- a constant desire and goal to produce an ever-increasing quality of both products and services to the school's and/or school district's customers

FINAL COMMENTS

EQM has much to offer individual school's or school district's planners and decision makers, stakeholders, and customers. If skillfully planned and implemented, it can provide both a higher quality level of products, processes, and services; and it can provide a much better level of internal and external customers' satisfaction. It is not a quick fix, not a revolutionary idea. Indeed, it is a long-term evolutionary process that will ultimately change the culture of the school and/or school district [17].

This text has built upon a variety of dimensions, concepts, and content areas within the field. The dynamics of change in the first chapter laid the groundwork for the proposed systematic alteration of the school system. Chapters 2 and 3 provided a background of motivation and leadership theories that carry attitudinal and environmental implications for the individuals in the system. The identification of needs in Chapter 4 illustrated a prerequisite for achieving EQM; and the subsequent chapters on Effective Schools research, Outcome-Based Education, and School-Based Management outlined the basic components of each of these conceptual and restructuring areas, connecting them to the larger TQM and EQM structures. Quality Management Basics in Chapter 8 provided a systematic framework for the combined restructuring models presented in Chapter 9. The QM connections with strategic and tactical planning were outlined and affirmed in Chapter 10.

Reviewing the key concepts of QM, SBM, OBE, Effective Schools, and strategic and tactical planning, we find that a complementary approach of these concepts will allow the development of a holistic approach to positive systematic and transformational change in schools, one that capitalizes upon the cornerstone concepts that have preceded it. The resulting Educational Quality Management system can merge, build upon, and strengthen its component change efforts and can serve as a synergistic, durable model and catalyst for twenty-first century school improvement.

REFERENCES

1. Herman, J. J. 1993. *Holistic Quality: Managing, Restructuring, Empowering Schools.* Newbury Park, CA: Corwin Press, Inc., a Sage Publications Company.
2. Herman, J. J. and J. L. Herman. In press. *Making Change Happen.* Newbury Park, CA: Corwin Press, Inc., a Sage Publications Company.
3. Kaufman, R. and D. Zahn. 1993. *Quality Management Plus: The Continuous Improvement of Education.* Newbury Park, CA: Corwin Press, Inc., a Sage Publications Company.
4. Rhodes, L. A. 1990. "Why Quality Is within Our Grasp . . . If We Reach," *School Administrator,* 47(10):31–34.
5. Axland, S. 1993. "Forecasting the Future of Quality," *Quality Progress,* 26(2):21–25.
6. Kaufman, R. and J. J. Herman. 1989. "Planning That Fits Every District: Three Choices Help Define Your Plan's Scope," *The School Administrator,* 46(8):17–19.
7. Herman, J. J. and J. L. Herman. 1991. *The Positive Development of Human Resources and School District Organizations.* Lancaster, PA: Technomic Publishing Company, Inc., pp. 19–20.
8. Kaufman, R. and J. J. Herman. 1991. *Strategic Planning in Education.* Lancaster, PA: Technomic Publishing Company, Inc., p. 246.
9. Bradley, L. H. 1993. *Total Quality Management for Schools.* Lancaster, PA: Technomic Publishing Company, Inc., pp. 228–230.
10. Herman, J. J. and J. L. Herman. 1993. *School-Based Management: Current Thinking and Practice.* Springfield, IL: Charles C. Thomas, Publishers, Inc., pp. 228–230.
11. Herman, J. J. 1992. "Strategic Planning: Reasons for Failed Attempts," *Educational Planning,* 8(3):36–40.
12. Rhodes, L. A. 1990. "Beyond Your Beliefs: Quantum Leaps Toward Quality Schools," *School Administrator,* 47(10):23–26.
13. Kaufman, R. and J. J. Herman. 1991. "Strategic Planning for a Better Society," *Educational Leadership,* 48(7):4–8.
14. Herman, 1993. *Holistic Quality.*
15. Kaufman, R. J., J. J. Herman and K. Watters. Forthcoming. *Planning Educational Systems: What, When, How.* Lancaster, PA: Technomic Publishing Co., Inc.
16. Herman, J. J. 1989. "Strategic Planning—One of the Changing Leadership Roles of the Principal," *The Clearing House,* 63(2):56–58.
17. Herman and Herman, in press.

Abernathy, P. E. and R. W. Serfass. 1992. "One District's Improvement Quality Story," *Educational Leadership,* 50(3):14–17.

Abrams, J. D. 1985. "Making Outcome-Based Education Work," *Educational Leadership,* 43(1):30–32.

Anderson, B. L. 1993. "The Stages of Systemic Change," *Educational Leadership,* 51(1):14–17.

Axland, S. 1993. "Forecasting the Future of Quality," *Quality Progress,* 26(2):21–25.

Barrow, J. W. 1993. "Does Total Quality Management Equal Organizational Learning?" *Quality Progress,* 26(7):39–44.

Barth, R. 1990. *Improving Schools from Within.* San Francisco, CA: Jossey-Bass, Publishers, p. 145.

Bennis, W. 1969. *Organizational Development: Its Nature, Origins and Prospects.* Reading, MA: Addison-Wesley Publishing Company, p. 2.

Betts, F. 1992. "How Systems Thinking Applies to Education," *Educational Leadership,* 50(3):38–41.

Bonstingl, J. J. 1992. "The Quality Revolution in Education," *Educational Leadership,* 50(3):4–9.

Bonstingl, J. J. 1992. *Schools of Quality: An Introduction to Total Quality Management in Education.* Alexandria, VA: Association for Supervision and Curriculum Development, pp. 42–43.

Bonstingl, J. J. 1993. "The Quality Movement: What's It Really About?" *Educational Leadership,* 51(1):66.

Boyd, W. L. 1990. "Balancing Control and Autonomy in School Reform: The Politics of Perestroika," in *The Educational Reform Movement of the 1980's,* J. Murphy (ed.), Berkeley, CA: McCutchan Publishing Corporation, pp. 88–89, 94.

Bradley, L. H. 1993. *Total Quality Management for Schools.* Lancaster, PA: Technomic Publishing Company, Inc., pp. 228–230.

Bragar, J. 1992. "The Customer-Focused Quality Leader," *Quality Progress,* 25(5):51–54.

Brookover, W. et al. 1982. *Creating Effective Schools: An Inservice Program for Enhancing School Learning Climate and Achievement.* Holmes Beach, FL: Learning Publications, Inc.

Byrnes, L. 1993. "Creating World-Class Teacher Education Programs with TQM," *TQM in Higher Education,* 2(1):1–2.

Carnall, C. 1986. "Managing Strategic Change: An Integrated Approach," *Long Range Planning,* 19(6):105–115.

Caroselli, M. 1992. *Quality-Driven Designs.* San Diego, CA: Pfeiffer and Company, pp. 67–72.

Case, T., R. Vandenberg and P. Meredith. 1990. "Internal and External Change Agents," *Leadership and Organization Development Journal,* 11(1):4–15.

Cawelti, G. 1987. "Strategic Planning for Curricular Reform," *Phi Kappa Phi Journal,* 67:29–31.

Champlin, J. 1991. "A Powerful Tool for School Transformation," *School Administrator,* 48(9):34.

Chaudron, D. 1992. "HR and TQM: All Aboard!" *HR Focus,* 69(11):1, 6.

Conner, D. and S. Hughes. 1988. "Architects of the Future – Managing Change," *CUPA Journal,* 39(4):15–18.

Cross, R. 1987. "Strategic Planning: What It Can and Can't Do," *Advanced Management Journal,* 52:13–16.

David, J. L. 1989. "Synthesis of Research on School-Based Management," *Educational Leadership,* 46(8):45–53.

Dinklocker, C. 1992. "Our Deming Users' Group," *Educational Leadership,* 50(3):32.

Duden, N. 1993. "A Move from Effective to Quality," *School Administrator,* 50(5):18–21.

Dutton, J. and R. Duncan. 1987. "The Influence of the Strategic Planning Process on Strategic Change," *Strategic Management Journal,* 8:103–119.

Evans, R. 1993. "The Human Face of Reform," *Educational Leadership,* 51(1):19–23.

Fields, J. C. 1993. "Unlocking the Paralysis of Will: Leaders Can Use School Efficacy to Unleash a 'Can-Do' Spirit," *Educational Leadership,* 50(5):9–13.

Fitzpatrick, K. A. 1991. "Restructuring to Achieve Outcomes of Significance for All Students: A Progress Report from Township High School District 214," *Outcomes: A Quarterly Newsletter of the Network for Outcome Based Schools.* Johnson City, NY (Winter):14–22.

Freeston, K. R. 1992. "Getting Started with TQM," *Educational Leadership,* 50(3):10–13.

Friedland, S. 1992. "Building Student Self-Esteem for School Improvement," *NASSP Bulletin,* 76(540):96–102.

Gilad, B. and T. Gilad. 1985. "Strategic Planning: Improving the Input," *Management Planning,* 33:10–13.

Gray, R., N. Hobar, R. Gagrys and C. Zimmerman. 1992. *The Total Quality Educator: Adapting Total Quality Management to Education,* Vol. 1 of the *Total Quality Education Trilogy.* Cockeysville, MD: Workforce 2000, Inc.

Gummer, B. 1990. "Managing Organizational Cultures: Management Science or Management Ideology?" *Administration in Social Work,* 14(1):135–153.

Hall, G. E. and S. M. Hord. 1987. *Change in Schools: Facilitating the Process.* Albany, NY: State University of New York Press, p. 51.

Hampton, D. R., C. E. Summer and R. A. Webber. 1987. *Organizational Behavior and the Practice of Management.* Glenview, IL: Scott, Foresman and Company, pp. 44, 559–575, 577–578, 586–592, 595–596.

Harvey, T. 1990. *Checklist for Change: A Pragmatic Approach to Creating and Controlling Change.* Boston, MA: Allyn and Bacon.

Herman, J. J. 1988. "Map the Trip to Your District's Future," *The School Administrator,* 45(9):16, 18, 23.

Herman, J. J. 1989. "A Decision-Making Model: Site-Based Communications Governance Committees," *NASSP Bulletin,* 73(521):61–66.

Herman, J. J. 1989. "External and Internal Scanning: Identifying Variables That Affect Your School," *NASSP Bulletin,* 73(520):48–52.

Herman, J. J. 1989. "Site-Based Management: Creating a Vision and Mission Statement," *NASSP Bulletin,* 73(519):79–83.

Herman, J. J. 1989. "Strategic Planning—One of the Changing Leadership Roles of the Principal," *The Clearing House,* 63(2):56–58.

Herman, J. J. 1989. "A Vision for the Future: Site-Based Strategic Planning," *NASSP Bulletin,* 73(518):23–27.

Herman, J. J. 1990. "Action Plans to Make Your Vision a Reality," *NASSP Bulletin,* 74(523):14–17.

Herman, J. J. 1990. "School-Based Management," *Instructional Leader* (journal of the Texas Elementary and Supervisors Association), 3(4):1–5.

Herman, J. J. 1990. "School Based Management: A Checklist of Things to Consider," *NASSP Bulletin,* 74(527):67–71.

Herman, J. J. 1991. "Confronting 'HOT' Issues Will Test President's Leadership Skills," *Michigan Association of School Boards Journal* (July/August):14, 15, 26, 29.

Herman, J. J. 1991. "Coping with Conflict," *The American School Board Journal,* 178(8):26–28.

Herman, J. J. 1991. "Prerequisites for Instructional Leadership," in *Instructional Leadership Handbook, Second Edition.* Reston, VA: National Association of Secondary School Principals, pp. 99–103.

Herman, J. J. 1991. in "School-Based Management: An Introduction," *School-Based Management: Theory and Practice.* Reston, VA: National Association of Secondary Principals, pp. v–vii.

Herman, J. J. 1992. "Don't Do It Yourself: Delegation," *Executive Educator,* 14(11):26–27.

Herman, J. J. 1992. "Key Steps to Develop School Governance Teams," *The School Administrator,* 49(1):34–35.

Herman, J. J. 1992. "School-Based Management: Sharing the Resource Decisions," *NASSP Bulletin,* 76(545):102–105.

Herman, J. J. 1992. "School-Based Management: Staffing and Budget Expenditures," *School Business Affairs,* 58(12):24–25.

Herman, J. J. 1992. "Strategic Planning: Reasons for Failed Attempts," *Educational Planning,* 8(3):36–40.

Herman, J. J. 1992. "Total Quality Management Basics: TQM Comes to School," *School Business Affairs,* 58(4):20–28.

Herman, J. J. 1993. *Holistic Quality: Managing, Restructuring, Empowering Schools.* Newbury Park, CA: Corwin Press, Inc., a Sage Publications Company.

Herman, J. J. 1993. "Is TQM for Me? A Decision-Making Interrogatory," *School Business Affairs,* 59(4):28–30.

Herman, J. J. 1993. "School-Based Management," *Educational Facilities Planner,* 31(1):30.

Herman, J. J. 1993. "Total Quality Management," *Educational Facilities Planner,* 31(1):30.

Herman, J. J. and J. L. Herman. 1991. *The Positive Development of Human Resources and School District Organizations.* Lancaster, PA: Technomic Publishing Company, Inc., pp. 19–20, 228–230.

Herman, J. J. and J. L. Herman. 1991. "Business Officials and School-Based Management," *School Business Affairs,* 57(11):34–37.

Herman, J. J. and J. L. Herman. 1992. "Educational Administration: School-Based Management," *The Clearing House,* 65(5):261–263.

Herman, J. J. and J. L. Herman. 1993. *School-Based Management: Current Thinking and Practice.* Springfield, IL: Charles C. Thomas Publisher, pp. 30–34, 228–230.

Herman, J. L. and J. J. Herman. 1993. "A State-by-State Snapshot of School-Based Management Practices," *International Journal of Educational Reform,* 2(3):256–262.

Herman, J. J. and J. L. Herman. In press. *Making Change Happen.* Newbury Park, CA: Corwin Press, Inc., a Sage Publications Company.

Herman, J. J. and R. Kaufman. 1991. "Making the Mega Plan," *The American School Board Journal,* 178(5):24–25, 41.

Herman, J. J. and G. Megiveron. 1987. "Administrative Magic: Turn Bureaucrats into Managers," *The American School Board Journal,* 174(2):32.

Herman, J. J. and G. Megiveron. 1993. *Collective Bargaining in Education: Win/Win, Win/Lose, Lose/Lose.* Lancaster, PA: Technomic Publishing Co., Inc.

Hill, P. T., J. J. Bonan and K. Warner. 1992. "Uplifting Education," *National School Board Journal,* 179(3):21–25.

Hill, W. J. 1992. "Value through Quality," *Quality Progress,* 25(5):31–34.

Hixson, J. and K. Lovelace. 1992. "Total Quality Management's Challenge to Urban Schools," *Educational Leadership,* 50(3):24–27.

Hobbs, M. E. and G. Bailey. 1987. "Outcome-Based Education Promises Higher Student Achievement and Less Stress for the Principal," *North Central Association Quarterly,* 61(3):406–411.

Holzman, M. 1993. "What Is Systemic Change?" *Educational Leadership,* 51(1):18.

Howlett, P. 1987. "Issue Management: Passing Fad or Ultimate Solution?" *Thrust for Educational Leadership,* 6(4):8–10.

Hoy, W. K. and C. G. Miskel. 1987. *Educational Administration, Third Edition.* New York, NY: Random House, pp. 176, 250–251, 271–272.

Isaacson, N. and J. Bamburg. 1992. "Can Schools Become Learning Organizations?" *Educational Leadership,* 50(3):42–44.

Ishikawa, K. 1992. As cited in J. J. Bonstingl, *Schools of Quality: An Introduction to Total Quality Management in Education.* Alexandria, VA: Association for Supervision and Curriculum Development, p. 17.

Jablonski, J. R. 1992. *Implementing TQM: Competing in the Nineties through Total Quality Management, Second Edition.* San Diego, CA: Pfeiffer & Company, pp. 67–72.

Johnson, R. S. 1993. "TQM: Leadership for the Quality Transformation, Part 3," *Quality Progress,* 26(3):91–94.

Johnson, R. S. 1993. "TQM: Leadership for the Quality Transformation, Part 5," *Quality Progress,* 26(5):83–86.

Kanter, R. 1987. "Managing Traumatic Change: Avoiding the 'Unlucky 13,' " *Management Review,* 76(5):23–24.

Kaufman, R. 1988. *Planninng Educational Systems: A Results-Based Approach.* Lancaster, PA: Technomic Publishing Company, Inc.

Kaufman, R. and J. J. Herman. 1989. "Planning That Fits Every District: Three Choices Help Define Your Plan's Scope," *The School Administrator,* 46(8):17–19.

Kaufman, R. and J. J. Herman. 1991. "Strategic Planning for a Better Society," *Educational Leadership,* 48(7):4–8.

Kaufman, R. and J. Herman. 1991. *Strategic Planning in Education.* Lancaster, PA: Technomic Publishing Company, Inc., pp. 89–108, 246.

Kaufman, R. and A. Hirumi. 1992. "Ten Steps to 'TQM Plus,' " *Educational Leadership,* 50(3):33–34.

Kaufman, R. and D. Zahn. 1993. *Quality Management Plus: The Continuous Improvement of Education.* Newbury Park, CA: Corwin Press, Inc., a Sage Publications Company.

Kaufman, R., J. J. Herman and K. Watters. Forthcoming. *Planning Educational Systems: What, When, How.* Lancaster, PA: Technomic Publishing Company, Inc.

Killion, J. P. and B. Kaylor. 1991. "Follow-Up: The Key to Training for Transfer," *Journal of Staff Development,* 12(1):64–67.

Kilmann, R. 1985. "Managing All Barriers to Organizational Success," *Training and Development Journal,* 39(9):64–72.

King, J. A. and K. M. Evans. 1991. "Can We Achieve Outcome-Based Education?" *Education Leadership,* 49(2):73–75.

Kinlaw, D. C. 1992. *Continuous Improvement and Measurement for Total Quality.* San Diego, CA: Pfeiffer & Company, p. 82.

Knight, T. 1985. "Use Strategic Planning to Catapult Ideas into Action," *Executive Educator,* 7:21–22.

Kulieke, M. J. 1991. "Assessing Outcomes of Significance," *Outcomes: A Quarterly Newsletter of the Network for Outcome Based Schools,* Johnson City, NY (Winter):25–29.

Lane, J. and E. Epps (ed.). 1992. *Restructuring the Schools: Problems and Prospects.* Berkeley, CA: McCutchan Publishing Corporation.

Lasher, G. C. 1993. "Quality Schools on a Shoestring," *Thrust for Educational Leadership,* 22(4):8–12.

Lawrie, J. 1990. "The ABC's of Change Management," *Training and Development Journal,* 44(3):87–89.

Lenz, R. and M. Lyles. 1986. "Managing Human Problems in Strategic Planning Systems," *Journal of Business Strategy,* 6:57–66.

Leonard-Barton, D. 1988. "Implementation Characteristics of Organizational Innovations," *Communication Research,* 15(5):603–631.

Levine, D. 1991. "Creating Effective Schools: Findings and Implications for Research and Practice," *Phi Delta Kappan,* 72(5):389–393.

Levinson, H. J. and C. Dehont. 1992. "Leading to Quality," *Quality Progress,* 25(5):55–60.

Lewis, J., Jr. 1989. *Implementing School-Based Management by Empowering Teachers.* Westbury, NY: J. L. Wilkerson Publishing Co.

Lezotte, L. 1989. *Effective Schools Research Abstracts.* Okemos, MI: Effective Schools Products.

Lezotte, L. W. (speaker). 1989. *Effective Schools Videotapes* (videotape recordings). Okemos, MI: Effective Schools Products.

McCune, S. 1986. *A Guide to Strategic Planning for Educators.* Alexandria, VA: Association for Supervision and Curriculum Development.

McEwen, N., C. Carmichael, D. Short and A. Steel. 1988. "Managing Organizational Change—A Strategic Approach," *Long Range Planning,* 21(6):71–78.

Mojkowski, C. 1991. *Developing Leaders for Restructuring Schools: New Habits of Mind and Heart.* Washington, DC: National LEADership Network Study Group on Restructuring Schools, p. 49.

Morrisey, G., P. Below and B. Acomb. 1988. *The Executive Guide to Operational Planning.* San Francisco, CA: Jossey-Bass, Inc.

NASSP. 1991. *School-Based Management: Theory and Practice.* Reston, VA: National Association of Secondary School Principals.

Newman, F. et al. 1991. *National Center on Effective Secondary Schools' Final Report on OERI Grant No. G-00869007.* Madison, WI: Wisconsin Center for Education Research.

Nyland, L. 1991. "One District's Journey to Success with Outcome-Based Education," *School Administrator,* 48(9):29, 31–32, 34–35.

Outcomes. 1991. "Criteria for Outcome-Based Education," *Outcomes: A Quarterly Newsletter of the Network for Outcome Based Schools.* Johnson City, NY (Spring):5.

Patterson, J. L. 1993. *Leadership for Tomorrow's Schools.* Alexandria, VA: Association for Supervision and Curriculum Development, pp. 42–43.

Peregrine, P. 1993. "Total Quality Assessment Programs for Schools," paper presented at the *Annual Meeting of the American Association of School Administrators,* Orlando, Florida, February 1993.

Pfeiffer, J. (ed.). *Strategic Planning: Selected Readings.* San Diego, CA: University Associates, Inc.

Reiner, C. A. and H. Morris. 1987. "Leadership Development," in *Training and Development Handbook, Third Edition,* Robert L. Craig (ed.), New York, NY: McGraw-Hill, pp. 523–524.

Rhodes, L. A. 1990. "Beyond Your Beliefs: Quantum Leaps Towards Quality Schools," *School Administrator,* 47(11):23–26.

Rhodes, L. A. 1990. "Why Quality Is within Our Grasp . . . If We Reach," *School Administrator,* 47(10):31–34.

Rubin, S. E. and W. G. Spady. 1984. "Achieving Excellence through Outcome-Based Instructional Delivery," *Educational Leadership,* 41(8):37–44.

Rush, H. M. F. 1987. "The Behavioral Sciences," in *Training and Development Handbook, Third Edition,* Robert L. Craig (ed.), New York, NY: McGraw-Hill, pp. 135–167.

Scarr, L. E. 1992. "Using Self-Regulating Work Teams," *Educational Leadership,* 50(3):68–70.

Schenkat, R. 1993. "Deming's Quality: Our Last but Best Hope," *Educational Leadership,* 51(1):64–65.

Schiller, R. E. and C. W. Freed. 1992. "Who Will Be at the Leadership Helm in the 1990's?" *The School Administrator,* 49(3):46–47.

Schlechty, P. C. 1990. *Schools for the Twenty-First Century.* San Francisco, CA: Jossey-Bass, Publishers, pp. 145–146.

Schleisman, K. E. and J. A. King. 1990. "Making Sense of Outcome-Based Education: Where Did It Come from, and What Is It?" (research report #7). Minneapolis, MN: Center for Applied Research and Educational Improvement.

Schmoker, M. and R. B. Wilson. 1993. "Adapting Total Quality Doesn't Mean 'Turning Learning into a Business,' " *Educational Leadership,* 51(1):62–63.

Schmoker, M. and R. B. Wilson. 1993. "Transforming Schools through Total Quality Education," *Phi Delta Kappan*, 74(5):389–395.

Siu-Runyon, Y. and S. J. Heart. 1992. "The Management Manifesto," *Executive Educator*, 14(1):23–26.

Smith, A. K. 1993. "Total Quality Management in the Public Sector, Part 1," *Quality Progress*, 26(6):45–50.

Smith, C. A. 1992. "Teams Building Teams: TQM and Classified Personnel Selection," *School Business Affairs*, 58(11):27–29.

Spady, W. G. 1988. "Organizing for Results: The Basis of Authentic Restructuring and Reform," *Educational Leadership*, 46(2):4–8.

Spady, W. P. and K. J. Marshall. 1991. "Beyond Traditional Outcome-Based Education," *Educational Leadership*, 49(2):67–72.

Tregoe, B. and P. Tobia. 1990. "An Action-Oriented Approach to Strategy," *The Journal of Business Strategy*, 1(1):16–21.

Veninga, R. 1987. "In Search of Excellence: Practical Strategies for Managing Change in Environmental Health," *Journal of Environmental Health*, 50(1):4–7.

Vickery, T. R. 1990. "ODDM: A Workable Model for Total School Improvement," *Educational Leadership*, 47(7):67–70.

Wagner, T. 1993. "Systemic Change: Rethinking the Purpose of School," *Educational Leadership*, 51(1):24–28.

Wiener, Y. 1988. "Forms of Value Systems: A Focus on Organizational Effectiveness and Cultural Change and Maintenance," *Academy of Management Review*, 13(4):534–545.

Willis, S. 1993. "Creating 'Total Quality' Schools," *Association of Supervision and Curriculum Development Update*, 35(2):1, 4–5.

Zemke, R. 1993. "A Bluffer's Guide to TQM," *Training*, 30(4):48–55.

Zlatos, B. 1993. "Outcomes-Based Outrage," *Executive Educator*, 15(9):12–16.